Teaching Guitar

An In-Depth Guide to Making a Living as a Professional Guitar Teacher

JODY FISHER

*Alfred, the leader in educational publishing,
and the National Guitar Workshop,
one of America's finest guitar schools, have joined
forces to bring you the best, most progressive
educational tools possible. We hope you will enjoy
this book and encourage you to look for
other fine products from Alfred and the
National Guitar Workshop.*

ISBN 0-7390-3745-5 (Book & CD)

*This book was acquired, edited and produced
by Workshop Arts, Inc., the publishing arm of
the National Guitar Workshop.
Nathaniel Gunod, managing and acquisitions editor
Burgess Speed, editor
Ante Gelo, music typesetter
Timothy Phelps and Justin Perillo, interior design
CD recorded at Studio 9, Ontario, California.
Cover photographs by Timothy Phelps and Burgess Speed.
Interior photographs by Timothy Phelps and Burgess Speed; others courtesy of the National Guitar Workshop.*

TABLE OF CONTENTS

About the Author 4

Introduction 5

Chapter One: Personal Skills 6
   Are You a Strong Player? 6
   Can You Teach? 8
   Building Confidence (Yours and Your Student's) 9
   Professionalism 10

Chapter Two: Types of Teaching 12
   One-on-One Lessons 12
   Classroom Teaching 13
   Clinics 15

Chapter Three: Teaching Environments 16
   Your Own Teaching Studio 16
   Teaching in Your Home 17
   Teaching in a Music Store 18
   Teaching in the Student's Home 19
   Telephone Lessons 19
   Teaching at a College or University 20
   Other Teaching Situations 26

Chapter Four: What You Will Need 28
   Office Supplies 28
   Studio/Teaching Supplies 29
   Musical Gear 31

Chapter Five: The Biz 32
   Advertising and Attracting Students..32
   Keeping Student Records 33
   Bookkeeping...36
   Promotion 38
   Selling Books, CDs and Other Supplies 39
   Attendance and Cancellation Policies 40
   Generating Additional Income 41

Chapter Six: Basic Teaching Chops 42
   Personality..42
   The First Lesson 42
   Sizing Up Your Student 42
   Teaching Different Age Groups 43
   Under-Teaching 45
   Teaching Good Practice Habits..45
   Dealing with Difficult Students 46
   Encouragement and Criticism 46
   Diagnostics: Targeting a Student's Difficulties 46

Chapter Seven: Basic Instructions for All Styles 47
   Posture 47
   Holding the Guitar 47
   Using a Strap 48
   Left-Hand Position and Fingering 48
   Basic Pick-Style Technique 48
   Basic Fingerstyle Technique 49
   Reading Standard Music Notation 49
   Reading TAB 49
   Tuning Options 49

Chapter Eight: Teaching Folk Guitar 50
   Learning Basic Chords 50
   Strumming Patterns and Chord Changes 52
   Fingerpicking 54

Chapter Nine: Teaching Blues Guitar 57
   Barre Chords 57
   9th Chords 60
   The Blues Progression 61
   Blues Rhythms 64
   Scales for Blues 66
   Starting to Improvise 69
   Experimenting with Time 69
   Learning and Using Licks 70
   Other Related Skills for Blues Guitar Students 72
   Learning Blues Songs 72

Chapter Ten: Teaching Rock Guitar 73
   Common Chords Used in Rock Guitar 73
   Rock Progressions 76
   Rock Rhythm Patterns 83
   Scales for Rock 84
   Rock Licks 87
   Other Related Topics for Rock Students 87

Chapter Eleven: Teaching Jazz Guitar 88
   Teaching Chordal Concepts 88
   Improvisation Concepts 92
   Other Areas of Study for Jazz Students 95

ABOUT THE CD

A compact disc is included with this book. It features:

- **Musical examples.**

- **Backing tracks**—with full rhythm section—for your students to improvise over.
  These are in the chapters: Teaching Blues Guitar (page 69), Teaching Rock Guitar (page 86) and Teaching Jazz Guitar (page 93).

- **Helpful forms for bookkeeping and maintaining student records.** Instructions for accessing these spreadsheet files for your computer are on pages 34 and 37.

The symbol at top left appears next to every example and backing track on the CD. The number below the symbol corresponds directly to the CD track number. Track 1 provides tuning notes for your guitar.

ABOUT THE AUTHOR

Jody Fisher has worked professionally in virtually all styles of music during his career, from straight-ahead and contemporary jazz to rock 'n' roll, country and pop. For several years, he was a director of the National Guitar Workshop. He also taught Guitar and Jazz Studies at both the University of Redlands and Idyllwild School of Music and the Arts (ISOMATA). He is an active performer in the Southern California area, where he maintains a busy private teaching practice.

PHOTO BY BRIAN MAURER

Other instructional materials by Jody Fisher:

30-Day Guitar Workout (Alfred/National Guitar Workshop—Book #17867)

Chord and Scale Finder (Alfred/National Guitar Workshop—Book #14148)

Ear Training for the Contemporary Guitarist (Alfred/National Guitar Workshop—Book & CD #19370)

Jazz Guitar Christmas Solos (Alfred/National Guitar Workshop—Book & CD #14869)

Jazz Guitar Masterclass (with Joe Diorio, Mark Whitfield, Ron Escheté, Scott Henderson and Steve Khan) (Alfred/National Guitar Workshop—Book #14827)

Jazz Skills (National Guitar Workshop—Book & CD #07-1012)

Rhythm Guitar Encyclopedia (Alfred/National Guitar Workshop—Book & 2 CDs #14838)

Stand Alone Tracks: Smooth Jazz (Alfred/National Guitar Workshop—Book & CD #17808)

The Complete Jazz Method:

    Beginning Jazz Guitar (Alfred/National Guitar Workshop—Book & CD #14120)

    Intermediate Jazz Guitar (Alfred/National Guitar Workshop—Book & CD #14123)

    Mastering Jazz Guitar: Chord/Melody (Alfred/National Guitar Workshop—Book & CD #14126)

    Mastering Jazz Guitar: Improvisation (Alfred/National Guitar Workshop—Book & CD #14129)

The Guitar Mode Encyclopedia (Alfred/National Guitar Workshop—Book #4445)

Jazz Guitar Harmony (Alfred/National Guitar Workshop—Book & CD #20440)

The Art of Solo Guitar, Book 1 (National Guitar Workshop—Book & CD #07-1053)

The Art of Solo Guitar, Book 2 (National Guitar Workshop—Book & CD #07-1056)

I Used to Play Guitar (Alfred/National Guitar Workshop—Book & CD #22683)

INTRODUCTION

When I was 16 years old, I received my first car. At the time, I didn't have a job or the financial means to maintain a car (or even buy gasoline). I had given a few guitar lessons to friends around the neighborhood, so I decided to try and get a job teaching guitar in the local music store. I walked in and told the woman behind the counter I was a guitar teacher and was looking for a place to teach. She was very friendly, but informed me they already had a "nice young man" teaching there. She told me to leave my phone number in case he ever left.

The next day, after coming home from school, I found a message on our kitchen counter. The store had called. The "nice young man" who had been teaching there had quit. I had a teaching gig!

I started with 40 students, meeting with each of them a half hour every week. The price of each lesson was three dollars (I got two and the store got one). Guitar instruction has come a long way since then. Teachers are better trained and there are books, CDs and videos to help students learn and practice in all kinds of new ways. We currently use technology that wasn't even dreamed about just a few years ago. However, there are still *many* things to consider when deciding if you want to teach guitar for a living.

It helps to be a good player, but you must also have good teaching chops. That's what this book is all about. We will cover topics such as setting up a teaching business, teaching in colleges and universities, teaching at home and teaching in music stores. There is advice for teaching beginners and advanced students, and suggested curriculums for most popular styles of guitar music. Because you will need a little business sense, we will also look at maintaining student records and bookkeeping.

While performing has always been my mainstay, teaching has always been a big part of my life. Through teaching, I have learned as much as (if not more than) my students about playing guitar and many other things.

Hopefully, you will have a similar experience.

The cliché, "teachers touch the future," is certainly true. As a teacher, you have the power to affect our cultural future. It's a big responsibility and a noble one at that.

This book is dedicated to all my students over the years, from whom I've learned so much.

Jody Fisher

CHAPTER ONE
PERSONAL SKILLS

Playing and teaching guitar are two very different skills. Many players assume that because they have acquired the skills to play or perform well, they automatically possess the skills to teach well. This is not always the case. The guitar world is filled with professional players who teach on the side for supplemental income. While anyone can understand the motivation, it is important to consider the whole picture. Teaching *only* for the money is unfair to both the student and yourself. Students can usually tell if you are being sincere during a lesson. If money is the prime objective, the students will know it, and you probably won't have them for very long. Being bored, watching the clock or not concentrating on the lesson are signs that teaching may not be right for you. You really have to enjoy teaching to do it well. Enthusiastic teachers breed good (and happy) students.

There are also teachers that never play professionally. While this is fine with beginning and intermediate students, more advanced students may prefer to study with teachers who are involved in the music industry as players and performers. Many want their information to come from teachers who are active in the field.

So you can see that being a good teacher, and making a living at it, requires the right motivation and life situation.

Before you can decide to teach guitar for a living, or as an avocation, you need to address two important questions: 1) Are you a strong player? 2) Can you teach?

ARE YOU A STRONG PLAYER?

OK, this is no time for modesty. It's time to size yourself up! Your students trust you to be both knowledgeable and skillful. Consider the following questions:

- Do you play at a consistent level 99% of the time?

- Are you missing information about the guitar that a teacher should know?

- Are you missing information about music or music theory that a teacher should know?

- Can you answer basic questions about equipment?

- How is your technique? Will students be inspired watching you play?

- Many teachers are very strong in one or two styles of music, but can still teach the basics of other styles too. What are *your* strongest styles? What other styles can you teach (if only to beginners)?

- Many students learn guitar so they can accompany themselves while singing. Do you sing? Can you sing?

- Can you read standard music notation? If you teach only TAB, you're not really helping to promote the art of guitar playing. Being an ace sight reader isn't necessary, but you should be competent.

- How's your improvising? In what styles can you teach improvisation?

- How well do you know the fretboard? Any trouble spots?

- Do you play pick style? Fingerstyle? Both? Can you teach both?

- Sometimes it is necessary to write out lessons by hand during a lesson. Can you write both standard music notation and TAB naturally and quickly? Students won't want to sit around in your studio if you struggle with these skills.

- Can you transcribe? How is your ear? Part of your job is teaching others to *hear*.

- How is your chord vocabulary?

Be honest with these questions. You don't have to be perfect to teach, but you should always be willing to update your skills and your knowledge. Why should your students feel inspired to learn if you don't?

"Why should your students feel inspired to learn if you don't?"

CAN YOU TEACH?

This book addresses teaching strategies for various styles of music and different kinds of students, but there are some basics that apply to all. Students will come to study with you for many reasons, which are not always musical. Depending on your teaching situation and environment, you will probably have students that are very serious about music. Others may only be looking for a hobby. Some students will desire a career in music, but most probably will not. You'll find there are as many reasons to study guitar as there are students. You will have to be flexible and open-minded. It is important to remember that not everyone is as serious about the guitar as you are; try to remember how you felt in your own "early" guitar days. Remember why you wanted to learn to play in the first place.

Now honestly answer the following questions:

- Do you like working with people?

- What age groups are you most comfortable with?

- Are you willing to teach the students what they want in addition to what you think they need?

- Are you a patient person?

- Are you willing to research answers to questions the student may have?

- Why do you want to teach? Money? Furthering the art? Fun?

- Do you have an organized approach to teaching various topics or do you just "wing it?"

- Often teachers have many students at the same stage of development. Can you teach the same topic repeatedly without getting bored or impatient?

- How will you approach discipline? How will you handle problem students? These are rare, but teachers have to deal with them occasionally.

- Can you inspire students to practice?

- Can you run your own business? You will have bookkeeping to do, as well as public relations, advertising and custodial work.

- Can you work alongside other teachers (as in a music store or school) without your ego getting in the way?

- Can you diagnose a student's problem? Is it a physical problem? A problem due to a lack of understanding? Something else?

- Can you offer positive criticism or suggestions without being condescending or sounding like a know-it-all? Diplomacy goes a *long* way!

- Can you begin your 10th lesson of the day with the same enthusiasm as you had for the first?

Once again, sainthood is not a requirement. No one is great all the time but the above questions illustrate the sort of personality traits good teachers should have.

BUILDING CONFIDENCE (YOURS AND YOUR STUDENT'S)

Feeling confident is important in any job, and teaching is no exception. Beginning students coming to you for their first lesson need to feel like you have the answers they need. Many times they have questioned whether they really have the ability to play a musical instrument. It's up to you to make them feel comfortable with the idea that, over time, they most certainly *will* acquire the skills they need to have fun playing.

It is natural at first to feel a little nervous in your new role as "teacher." Don't worry though, you will gradually become more and more comfortable. Also, when you begin to see your students make progress, your confidence will increase and you will feel a great sense of accomplishment. You also have to realize that most students (especially beginners) will look to you as the expert (even if it is your first day teaching).

You have a responsibility to confidently guide your students toward their goals. This does not mean you have to "know everything." Admitting you don't have all the answers can often increase a student's confidence and respect for you, especially if you offer to research their question and get back to them later.

Building up your students' confidence in themselves is one of the most important things you can do as a teacher. Their confidence level is directly related to their success in learning guitar. Your approach in these matters will vary considerably from student to student. Remember that you could be dealing with very different personality types every half-hour. For instance, if you are teaching in a music store where anyone can walk in and sign up for lessons, you could end up with a roster like this:

Monday

3:30–4:00	Nat Doe (high school student, wants to be a rock star)
4:00–4:30	Dave Doe (jr. high school student, would rather play soccer)
4:30–5:00	Paula Doe (third grader, short attention span)
5:00–5:30	Ian Doe (retired construction worker, missing a finger)
5:30–6:00	Nicole Doe (housewife, needs a hobby)
6:00–6:30	Jesse Doe (serious, did I say serious? I meant *serious* jazz student)
6:30–7:00	Barbara Doe (shows up because she thinks you're cute)
7:00–7:30	Trish Doe (really good fingerstylist)
7:30–8:00	Dennis Doe (wants to play the blues)
8:00–8:30	Dr. Matt Doe (thinks studying guitar will help him relax)
8:30–9:00	Dierdre Doe (has some poems she wants to put to music)

This is not far-fetched at all. A teacher has to relate to each student in a different way, based on his/her personality, age, life experience and interests. Each student has to walk away from their session believing they can successfully accomplish the week's lesson.

This is extremely rewarding work that can also be challenging. Maintaining a friendly and confident manner and cultivating the student's belief that he/she can succeed is a big part of the job.

PROFESSIONALISM

It is wrongly perceived that musicians can act or dress any way they wish. Stories of rock stars on tour and in everyday life fan these misconceptions. Actually, very few professional musicians could ever hope to make a living if they behaved that way. The truth is that people *do* expect you to be a little "cooler" than most folks. Yes, you can have your little quirks. You can dress to express. You can talk and act like a musician. But if you want to stay in business, you'll have to learn to relate to all kinds of people—and they'll need to be able to relate to you too.

Parents will leave their children with you. You need to appear (and be) trustworthy.

Students of the opposite gender need to feel like you are there to teach. "Hitting" on your students is never appreciated.

Junior high and high school students need to be able to relate to you. Don't try to jive them. They'll know.

Professional people want to study with teachers that take their craft and art very seriously.

Adult students who may be outstanding in other areas of life sometimes feel embarrassed or self-conscious if they are having trouble learning something new.

A good teacher will reassure them without going overboard and embarrassing them further.

"...if you want to stay in business, you'll have to learn to relate to all kinds of people—
and they'll need to be able to relate to you too."

A Few More Tips on Professionalism

- **Start and end your lessons on time.** It might seem like a nice thing to give a student a little extra time, but if it means your next student's lesson will start late, you'll probably run behind schedule the rest of the day. People lead busy lives and don't appreciate rushing to a lesson only to find you are running late. Now their lesson and the rest of their day or evening will be affected.

    Some teachers actually schedule an extra 10 or 15 minutes between lessons. This gives them a short break and pads the time slot in case a lesson lasts longer than it's supposed to. You can't schedule quite as many students in a day this way, but it can keep you a little saner.

- **Find polite, professional ways to ask for your payment.** "Well, it's pay day," or "time to pay the bills," can be casual and friendly ways to get the point across.

- **Find polite, professional ways to end the lesson.** "Time's Up!" probably doesn't make the student feel too great. All students want to feel like you care about them. "Well, that was fun. Do you think you have enough to work on this week? Any questions?" This shows you care but it's time to move on. Wrapping things up this way, five minutes before the end of the lesson, ensures you will have time to answer any questions they have and still begin the next lesson on time.

- **Dress casually** in most cases. Shirts that blare radical political or social beliefs or obscenities are not usually appreciated by students or parents. This is a sign of immaturity. Being a pro means you will most likely work in a variety of situations with a variety of people. You need to be appropriate.

- **Watch your language.** Different people have different standards. While teaching, it's best to play it safe and stick to topics and adjectives that most people deem socially acceptable.

- **Make notes about what your students are working on.** Glance at them before the student arrives so you don't begin the lesson with, "so, what are we working on...?"

- **Be consistent.** People arrange their schedules pretty tightly these days. One change, and the domino effect will take over. Yes, sometimes you may have to cancel a lesson, but try not to shuffle your students' schedules around excessively. If their lessons become a hassle, they will quit (especially beginners).

CHAPTER TWO
TYPES OF TEACHING

An area you need to consider is the *kind* of teaching you want to do. Does "one-on-one" teaching appeal to you? Teaching on a weekly basis? Monthly? What about classroom teaching? Are you capable of conducting special clinics? Many guitar teachers teach in a few different situations. While certain basics are common to all of these situations, each type of teaching requires specific skills.

ONE-ON-ONE LESSONS

One-on-one lessons are probably the most popular way to study the guitar. This arrangement allows the student to study privately with the instructor and progress at his/her own rate. For beginners and intermediate students these lessons usually occur once a week at a specified time. During the lesson, the previous week's assignment is reviewed and corrections, if needed, are suggested. Related questions are usually answered at this time. If the student's work shows that he/she is ready for new material, the teacher then introduces a new assignment.

Some students feel intimidated in a classroom situation. Private lessons offer, well, privacy. Some feel freer to ask questions and don't get as rattled over mistakes once they've become comfortable with their teacher. Another reason many people prefer private lessons is that the student has the teacher's undivided attention. Some students learn best (and often faster) this way.

Private lessons allow a teacher to better monitor the student's technique and level of understanding. In classroom teaching, it's easy to miss when someone is having a problem if you're not looking right at them. One-on-one lessons can be very intense. You may have to explain something many times and in many different ways until the student understands. Obviously, patience is a real necessity here.

You will also need endurance for this kind of teaching. Many teachers meet with 30–40 students on a weekly basis. This means there will be days when you may teach six or eight lessons in a row. Each student shows up expecting you to be at your best. You have to deliver—and this can sometimes be a challenge. Fatigue can set in and your voice can get tired or hoarse. You have to stay motivated and interested.

One great thing about private teaching is that you get to know your students better. Besides helping them, your life is enriched as well.

What to charge? Cost of living varies greatly from one location to another. It's probably best to get an idea of what other teachers charge in your area.

ADVANCED ONE-ON-ONE LESSONS BY APPOINTMENT

Many advanced students do not want a weekly guitar lesson. Instead, they may prefer to take longer, more involved lessons less frequently for very specific areas of study. Students at this level may not need weekly assignments anymore. They may just need someone to "open a door" for them occasionally. After these lessons, the students can practice and study until they feel ready to make another appointment with you.

While from a financial and scheduling standpoint these are not as consistent or reliable as weekly lessons, you may find that you really look forward to these sessions. It may be in these lessons that you are most challenged. Most teachers will tell you they can learn as much during a lesson as their student does.

Many teachers prefer to make these "appointment" lessons a little longer, usually anywhere from one to two hours depending on the student's need.

What to charge? Once again it depends on the standard rate in your area. If you are successful and your reputation grows you may be able to charge a higher fee.

CLASSROOM TEACHING

Classroom teaching is very different from one-on-one teaching. Classes exist in many different contexts. You'll find guitar classes in high schools, colleges, city park and recreation departments, YMCAs, churches and private organizations. Obviously, the requirements for teaching a university-level class differ from those needed to teach at the local Y, but there are still many things in common.

The reasons students take a guitar class vary widely. Music majors in college may be taking a required class for graduation. Non-majors may just need an extra unit or two and might not be taking the class otherwise. Students taking guitar classes at the Y or a local music store might just be looking for a good time in an enjoyable environment. While you may find an introverted student or two, guitar classes tend to attract folks who are comfortable in social situations.

Your professionalism must be in full force here, and your confidence level needs to be strong. Your class size could be anywhere from 3 to 45 students. In the first moments of class, the students are sizing you up and deciding how they feel about you. You must set the tone right from the beginning. Be natural—let your natural personality come out. Be relaxed and friendly, but let it be known you are in charge and know exactly what you're doing. Students can tell if you are insecure with your role as teacher in the classroom. If they doubt your authority, they may doubt your knowledge as well.

Maintaining control is extremely important. Control the workflow of each session. Be sure you are prepared with enough to do, but not too much. Class time will be limited, so you really can't linger as long as you might like on any given topic. If your class meets for a specific number of weeks, you will be expected to cover a certain amount of material in that time. It is necessary to plan ahead to accomplish these goals.

Maintaining control can also mean keeping the students orderly. The age of your students will determine the tactics you use to do this. Teaching young children is a lot different from teaching high school students, while teaching credit-courses at a college or conservatory is different still. Be sure you have the right temperament and personality for the age group you plan to teach.

Beginning guitar classes can be the most difficult to teach. Teaching the class how to tune their guitars can be a real challenge. Some teachers go around the class and tune each student's guitar individually. While this gives the instructor a chance to inspect everyone's instrument, it takes a lot of time. You could easily use half the class time doing this. While learning to tune by ear is important, you could show the class how to use an electronic tuner and leave one in the classroom for your students to use *before* class. This will save you much class time.

How do you give the proper amount of attention to each student? Much of the responsibility lies with the student. It is up to each person to ask questions and let you know when they do not understand something. You have to be on the lookout, too. You will get to know many of the students in your class. You will know to watch certain students for problems, based on how they have picked up previous concepts. Be sure to make eye contact a few times with each student during every class session. This makes the student feel that you care about their individual progress. Many instructors will have the students work on a few things on their own while he/she circulates through the room checking on everyone's progress.

Talk slowly and clearly in class. Be aware that each person seated before you is coming from a different life experience. It's up to you to try to connect with each student. You may not always accomplish this, but you must always give it your best shot.

Before moving on to new concepts be sure to ask if there are any questions. Always let the class know what you hope to accomplish during the session. Always recap previous information before moving on to new material.

"In the first moments of class, the students are sizing you up and deciding how they feel about you. You must set the tone right from the beginning. Be natural—let your natural personality come out. Be relaxed and friendly, but let it be known you are in charge and know exactly what you're doing."

CLINICS

Clinics, workshops and camps are usually run by schools or other institutions. Generally, these situations resemble the classroom scenario.

Students attending clinics are usually pretty serious, but it is possible to have students at all different levels of experience in attendance. It's important to address each student's interests as much as possible. Even when there are beginners, intermediate and advanced players in the same class, it is possible to cover topics from different levels. For instance, if you are discussing intervals, you might define and give very basic information to the beginners, teach how to recognize intervals by sight and by sound to the intermediate students and teach how to use intervals to create more modern sounds to the advanced folks. You could teach almost any subject this way.

Teachers that conduct a lot of clinics usually have a specialty that sets them apart from other teachers. If this is the kind of teaching situation you are looking for, be sure to market your class clearly so that students know exactly what will be covered. Make sure you have a strong handle on the information. Your credibility has to be solid.

"Students attending clinics are usually pretty serious, but it is possible to have students at all different levels of experience in attendance. Even when there are beginners, intermediate and advanced players in the same class, it is possible to cover topics from different levels."

CHAPTER THREE
TEACHING ENVIRONMENTS

There is a lot more to consider than simply choosing between teaching privately or in the classroom. Within the two categories are many possibilities. It is important to think about all of these teaching environments so you can start teaching in ways and in situations that are most comfortable and natural for you. Some guitar teachers work in more than one of these environments. At first, however, it is probably a good idea to stick to just one until your skills develop and your levels of experience and confidence increase.

YOUR OWN TEACHING STUDIO

Thoughts of self-employment fill most people's heads with visions of getting to do what you want, when you want. You can create your own schedule, work only the days you want and have complete control over your life. What's more, you don't have to "work for the man." Right?

Wrong! Nothing can be further from the truth. Most people who own their own business work pretty long hours each day. There are no guaranteed days off or vacations unless they create them. They also soon realize that they must take care of *all* the responsibilities themselves. When you run your own business, you are the CEO, the janitor and everyone else in between.

On the other hand, nothing beats dreaming up, creating and actually being in charge of your own career. Sure, you will be very busy, but at the end of the day, your success and accomplishments are all yours.

RENTING STUDIO AND OFFICE SPACE

People are more likely to view your teaching practice as a legitimate business when it is conducted at a professional facility. To rent a storefront or office space you'll need to consider the following:

- **How much space do you need?** There should be a reception area along with your actual teaching space. This is where students will wait for their lessons when they show up a little early, or where parents can wait for their kids during their lessons. You will need several chairs, possibly a couch and a table or two where you can stack magazines and other reading material. You'll need lighting as well. If you want to use this same area as an office, you will also need a desk, possibly a computer and all your other office supplies. This can be where students schedule and pay for their lessons. Of course, you'll want to decorate the place in a way that reflects your tastes and personality.

- **Will you be the only person teaching there?** If not, you will need separate studios for each teacher unless you schedule alternate teaching times and can share a single space. Often, guitar teachers who go this route will build their own partitions within the office. It's great if you have these skills (or some construction savvy friends) but if you don't, you'll have to add the cost of construction to your startup costs.

- **You will need additional space if you plan to sell products like books, strings, picks and other accessories.** If this is the case, you will need a display area with enough space to store inventory as well. You'll also have to have a cash register. Keep in mind that if you do sell products, you will be responsible for tracking and paying sales taxes and other related expenses. There is a fine line between having a teaching studio that sells a few items and opening a music store. If you really want to spend most of your time teaching, be careful about how many items you choose to sell. By the same token, you should carry the basics your students could need while taking their lessons. There will be broken strings and lost picks to replace, and new books to buy. Your students will expect to be able to purchase these items at your studio, so even if you're not selling to turn a profit, you should be able to provide these things for your students. It's cool if you break even in this area of your business.

- **Try to locate your studio where there is a lot of foot traffic.** Of course, highly desirable locations will cost more to rent and maintain, but you could end up with many more students as well. On the other hand, you will generally spend much less if you rent in a more industrial or residential part of town. You want to be easy to find. You'll need a business name and of course a sign. In addition to rent and startup costs your monthly overhead will include:

  - Utilities—gas, electric, etc.

  - Phone/internet services

  - Cleaning

  - Advertising

TEACHING IN YOUR HOME

There are advantages and disadvantages to teaching at home. Obviously, your startup costs are much lower because your "studio rent" is absorbed in your house payment, or monthly rent. Ideally, you should have an extra room in your house or apartment devoted to your business. You still need a waiting area and a place to take care of "business." Working at home is cool, but you have to be disciplined. Try not to take care of home duties when you should be working, and vice versa. If you sell supplies, you still need to take care of sales tax and all the governmental regulations.

It is also possible to deduct a part of your house payment or rent each year when you figure your taxes. Usually a percentage is deducted based on the square footage of your workspace. If you show a profit each year, this is perfectly legitimate. If not, the government considers your "business" more of a hobby and you may find it difficult to claim any expenses at all.

One of the most convenient aspects of teaching at home is that all your equipment is already there. Your guitars, music stands, amps, computer with appropriate programs, recording gear and repair supplies are readily available. Make sure to set up your work area so it looks professional. This shows your students (and their parents) that you're serious.

The three drawbacks to teaching at home are:

1. **People you do not know very well are walking in and out of your house** all the time. Once you get to know your students, things usually go fine. It is important to screen all possible students, however. You only have to take the students with whom you feel comfortable.

2. **It is more difficult to find new students** or replace those who have quit. In a music store or teaching studio there is generally "walk-in" traffic. Some of these folks will sign up for lessons. Stores and studios generally advertise or are listed in the yellow pages. This attracts traffic and sign-ups. This doesn't usually occur when you teach at home. Word of mouth is generally how home teachers get new students. Advertising is still an option, though.

3. **There is not much separation between your work life and your home life.** Some people have no problem with this, while others do. Remember, working at home means you could get business calls any time of the day and night. If students forget their lesson time, they could end up knocking on your door at inopportune times.

So it really depends on your goals, personality and situation in life.

TEACHING IN A MUSIC STORE

This is the best-case scenario for many teachers. Music stores have the teaching space, the utilities, the advertising, the supplies, the lesson policy and the walk-in traffic that teachers need. In addition to this, the whole environment is conducive to teaching guitar.

Sometimes the store sets the fee for the lessons. Other stores let the teachers determine their own fees. In any case, the store ends up with a percentage of the lesson fee, which is usually considered "rent" for the studio space and other perks. There is no standard percentage for this. Each store has its own policies. Some charge a lot for rent and, though this is rare, others charge nothing because the teacher draws customers into their store. Most stores, however, do seem to charge a fair rate.

If the store pushes their teaching program, teachers can expect to do quite well. New students sign up on a regular basis and those who leave are easily replaced. The teacher only has to show up on time and teach. It is also quite common for teachers in music stores to receive substantial discounts on equipment and supplies, which comes in pretty handy. Also, if you spend this much time in a music store you'll find it easier to keep up with all the new equipment and educational supplies coming out. Another perk is that people who want to hire musicians often call music stores for recommendations. The teachers often end up with these gigs.

Some disadvantages:

- If the store employs many other teachers, **there may not be enough studio space for everyone.** This means you may not be able to teach as often as you wish. On the other hand, if you are the only teacher, you stand to do quite well.

- **You have less control.** The store could change its policies regarding rent, lesson times, etc.

- **The store could be a very noisy place.** The noise could come from customers trying out equipment or even other teachers giving lessons. Of course, you are probably making noise as well.

Some teachers do pretty well financially by teaching in multiple stores in different areas. Except for studio rent and supplies, the overhead is very low.

TEACHING IN THE STUDENT'S HOME

Some teachers travel to the student's home for each lesson. While convenient for the student, this arrangement really drives up the cost of the lesson. Teachers must include the cost of transportation (gas, bus fare, etc.) along with the lesson fee. In addition, the travel time impacts how many students you can see in a day. Teachers generally charge quite a bit for this service. This is more popular in rural or very exclusive areas.

TELEPHONE LESSONS

This type of lesson is increasing in popularity. It is primarily intended for more advanced players. An hourly rate is charged according to the teacher's reputation, and the student generally sends a check by mail. Students who wish to study with a teacher who lives outside of their area find these lessons quite workable.

"Some teachers travel to the student's home for each lesson.
Teachers generally charge quite a bit for this service."

TEACHING AT A COLLEGE OR UNIVERSITY

Teaching guitar at a college or university can offer a comfortable and relatively stable life as a musician. Generally, full-time positions are salaried but you may be paid an hourly rate if you are teaching part-time. One advantage here is that if your student decides to miss a lesson, you will still be paid. In private teaching, you are responsible for finding and maintaining your student roster, taking care of the studio, the bookkeeping and all the rest. In a college, these duties are taken care of for you. Your primary job is to teach, and it usually comes along with quite a bit of respect from the students and the community as well. The length of your contract can range from a single semester (or quarter) to an open-ended full-time position. In some situations you may be able to earn tenure, which basically means you have a "lifetime" contract.

Still want to play gigs? It is not unusual for full-time college instructors to teach during the day and play gigs in the evening; while teaching part-time at a college is a great way to supplement performance income.

FULL-TIME POSITIONS

These positions almost always require advanced college degrees. Happily, we are living at a time when this is quite possible. Most colleges and universities offer degrees in music and guitar. You will need to earn the highest degree you can because there is a lot of competition. Most universities will require at least a master's degree. Earning a PhD will increase the odds for your success, of course. Community colleges require master's degrees as well. If a more academic life is your desire, plan on several years of formal training. What should your major be? It could be in guitar performance of course, but it could also be in education, music technology, composition, theory, music history, music therapy or even ethnomusicology.

Full-time positions are usually defined by teaching a certain number of units, or credits, per semester. This can vary from school to school, but as an example, to accumulate enough units you may be required to teach private or class guitar lessons in addition to theory classes or directing an ensemble. Full-time positions usually come with other duties and responsibilities as well. Most full-time professors are required to serve on various committees in addition to their teaching. These committees can decide issues as diverse as the department's budget, to incoming student auditions or instrument and equipment acquisition.

In addition, some schools require you to spend a certain number of hours in your office so students can meet with you. You will also participate in student auditions and juries, and possibly have a hand in curriculum development.

Most colleges offer guitar lessons to non-music majors as well. You may find yourself teaching a classroom full of engineering or literature majors. Some of these students may be quite interested in learning to play, but you'll also find those who just need the extra credit or two.

If your college offers an ensemble program you will spend time searching for (or writing) arrangements for your students. Many music departments expect you to travel to music competitions with your students, too. There will be papers to grade and tests to give. You will assign grades at the end of the term. Some students (and possibly their parents) may occasionally give you grief. You will also have students (and once again, their parents) who think you are the greatest. You will spend time recruiting new students because this is how you keep your department alive. This can be a lot of work and responsibility, so you can see there is much more than just class and rehearsal time involved. Most guitarists who choose this avenue really love teaching and working with people. This life can be extremely rewarding. You also get summers off.

Salaries are negotiable and based on your degree and level of experience. It also doesn't hurt to have had some instructional materials published or recordings released.

It should be mentioned that not all teaching institutions absolutely *require* that you have a degree. However, these situations are rare and becoming even more so as guitarists with degrees increase in number. Depending on where you live, state schools that usually require degrees can get around the policy by claiming "equivalency." This means that they are willing to hire a teacher who, while lacking a degree, qualifies in terms of experience or reputation. There are experts in every field who teach in colleges under this arrangement. Private colleges prefer instructors with degrees as well, but don't have to adhere to state requirements. It could be a little easier to claim equivalency at these schools. However, if you have the chance to earn the degree, do it! All departments in every school want a roster of professors who look great on paper. It helps to recruit students and attract funding. Remember that schools are businesses as well as institutions.

ADJUNCT PROFESSOR

Colleges and universities often hire part-time instructors to teach specialized topics. Guitar is just such a topic. Many band instructors at colleges play wind instruments and/or piano, but do not have any experience with the guitar. They *have* to hire a part-time professor for this. There are usually quite a few students interested in pursuing guitar studies. This rounds out the program and makes money for the music department. There are many adjunct guitar professors out there. Very few of them give up their positions and are hoping to eventually turn full-time. You will probably be paid on an hourly basis, and your contract will have to be renewed each semester depending on the number of students who sign up for your class. Sometimes a class "goes" and sometimes it doesn't. Quite a few adjunct professors have positions at more than one college and are usually very busy, at times teaching more than some full-time professors.

CREATING A SYLLABUS

Almost all colleges and universities require you to submit a syllabus, or class plan, for each class you teach. This tells both the school and students exactly what you plan to cover, and in how much time. Creating a great syllabus requires research and, most of all, experience. Most teachers tend to over-teach at first. It takes a few years of this kind of teaching to be able to realistically plan the amount of information you can cover in a semester. The course must be challenging, but not impossible.

Most syllabi start with the minimum requirements and a general description of the class. This is followed by a class-by-class listing of the topics that will be covered. Test dates and project deadlines are usually listed here as well. Here is a sample syllabus for a general 12-week (two meetings per week) jazz guitar class.

Class: Jazz Guitar 101

Prerequisite: Basic fretboard knowledge. Competent skills in either the blues or rock genres.

Description: This class meets twice a week for one 12-week semester. This beginning class covers scale construction and fingerings, chord theory, chord/scale relationships and fingerings, introductory improvisation, upper and lower neighbor tones, modes, arpeggios, technique and repertoire.

Three independent projects are required.

1. Term paper about the life of one well-known jazz guitarist.
2. Harmonic analysis of six standard tunes not covered in class.
3. Jazz performance reviews. The student must attend at least six live jazz performances during the course of the semester. A 500 word review is required for each. The six reviews will be submitted at the end of the semester along with the two independent projects listed above.

In addition, the student is expected to spend at least one hour per day listening to recordings of artists listed in the textbook.

Grades are based on satisfactory completion of all homework and projects. A thorough understanding of all topics covered is expected along with regular class attendance.

Week 1
   Session 1
   • How to Practice
   • Intervalic Relationships
   • The Circle of 5ths

   Session 2
   • Major Scale Construction
   • Major Scale Fingerings
      • 1st Position—E and A
      • 2nd Position—E
   • Quiz

Week 2

Session 3
- Major Scale Fingerings
  - 2nd Position—A
  - 4th Position—E and A
- Triad Theory

Session 4
- 1st Inversion Triads on Three String Sets
- 2nd Inversion Triads on Three String Sets
- 3rd Inversion Triads on Three String Sets
- Quiz

Week 3

Session 5
- Melodic Patterns
- Two Simple Songs

Session 6
- Extended Chord Theory
- Fingerings for Major 6th, 7th, 9th and 13th Chords
- Quiz

Week 4

Session 7
- Fingerings for Dominant 7th, 9th, 11th and 13th Chords
- Connecting Major Scale Fingerings

Session 8
- Fingerings for Minor 6th, 7th, 9th, 11th and 13th Chords
- Two Chord Etudes
- Midterm Exam

Week 5

Session 9
- The Harmonized Major Scale
- Horizontal Fingerings for the Harmonized Major Scale

Session 10
- Vertical Fingerings for the Harmonized Major Scale
- Three-Octave Major Scales
- Quiz

Week 6

<u>Session 11</u>
- Combined Fingerings for the Harmonized Major Scale
- Two-Chord Etudes

<u>Session 12</u>
- Roman Numerals and Transposition
- Memorizing Songs
- Test

Week 7

<u>Session 13</u>
- More About Roman Numerals and Transposition
- Single-Note Scale Technique

<u>Session 14</u>
- Major Scale Mode Theory
- Explanation of Parallel and Derivative Approaches
- Quiz

Week 8

<u>Session 15</u>
- Modal Practice Progressions
- How Jazz Works

<u>Session 16</u>
- Introduction to Arpeggios
- Introduction to Neighbor Tones
- Test

Week 9

<u>Session 17</u>
- Diatonic Arpeggios of the Major Scale—Theory
- Diatonic Arpeggios of the Major Scale—Fingerings (Three Sets)

<u>Session 18</u>
- Diatonic Arpeggios of the Major Scale—Fingerings (Three More Sets)
- Note Identification on the Fretboard
- Quiz

Week 10

Session 19

- Applying Lower Neighbor Tones
- Applying Upper Neighbor Tones

Session 20

- Surrounding Chord Tones with Upper and Lower Neighbor Tones
- Practice Progressions
- Quiz

Week 11

Session 21

- Repertoire Development—What Songs to Learn First?

Session 22

- Improvising: Coming Up with Ideas
- Learning Licks
- Quiz

Week 12

Session 23

- Review

Session 24

- Final Exam
- All Projects Due

*"Quite a few adjunct professors have positions at more than one college and are usually
very busy, at times teaching more than some full-time professors."*

OTHER TEACHING SITUATIONS

The teaching environments mentioned so far represent the most common situations. However, there may be other avenues to pursue as well. Consider the following:

CITY PARK AND RECREATION

Most cities and towns have a Park and Recreation department. Aside from activities like softball, soccer, arts and crafts and first aid classes, they commonly offer music classes as well. Generally, these classes meet once or twice a week, for six to eight weeks. Guitar classes are frequently listed in their brochures.

You can expect students from all walks of life in this situation. It's likely that adults, kids, teenagers and senior citizens will all end up in class together. The focus in these classes should be on having fun. Most folks who take "park 'n rec" classes are primarily looking for diversion. Concentrate on simple songs, chords, strums and fingerpicking. If your students enjoy the sessions they could sign up every time the class is offered. If your class turnout is good, the city may offer the class on a more regular basis.

CHURCHES

Churches and synagogues often offer classes for their members and congregations. You could take an entirely secular approach, or if you are well versed in religious and liturgical music, you could teach a class covering that kind of material. Another possibility is to offer classes for different age groups within the church. Situations like this are often good for picking up additional private students as well.

YMCA

The YMCA (and other private organizations like the Boys and Girls Clubs) is well known for the variety of classes it offers. It is usually just a matter of talking to the people in charge about offering a weekly class. The students pay the Y and the Y pays you. You might even be able to have continuing classes for students at various levels of ability. Offering classes aimed at different kinds of students will widen your reach and can keep you employed. Try a folk or rock class. Offer a class for those who want to accompany singing. Around Christmas time, try offering a class that teaches Christmas music. A class that teaches patriotic songs and Americana might work around the Fourth of July.

COMMUNITY COLLEGES

Landing a teaching position at a community college has been discussed previously, but many schools offer a variety of classes outside the "class-for-credit" structure. Check to see if your local community college has such a program. These classes are usually attended by unmatriculated students from the local community.

SENIOR CENTERS

Seniors look for ways to grow and enrich their lives. Retirement communities offer various classes and programs spanning many different subjects, including music. Be prepared to teach songs that were popular with previous generations. Aside from making a living, you'll be doing a good thing for the community.

ADULT EDUCATION

Check with your city administrators to see if your town offers an adult education program. Many towns do. Some programs only offer more "serious" classes such as English as a Second Language, Computers, Bookkeeping or even Basic Reading. However, many also offer a wide variety of "lighter" classes in art, drama and music.

INDEPENDENT SEMINARS AND WORKSHOPS

Even if you teach in a music store or college, you can still offer special classes on the side. Pick a specialized topic like slide playing, alternate tunings or anything else you can dream up, and hold a special evening class or workshop. Some of your regular students will probably sign up along with others as well. Advertise in the store or school you teach at to draw other teachers' students as well. You charge a fee for the class which covers handouts, books, etc.

MUSIC CAMP

Every summer there are music camps all over the world. Do a search and send a resume, picture and recording to every camp that appeals to you. Some music camps focus on a particular style of music, like folk or acoustic music. Others offer a full catalog of classes that range from folk and rock to classical and jazz. You will usually receive food and accommodations along with a summer paycheck.

A VERY NOVEL IDEA

Here's yet another idea. A famous acoustic guitarist from France opens his home (he lives on a farm) to students for six weeks at a time. The students eat, sleep, study and practice guitar the whole time they are in residence. The teacher gives a master class each week and sees each student privately in between. In this scenario, there are obviously *many* concerns, but it shows how you can take an idea and turn it into an interesting way to make a living teaching guitar.

CHAPTER FOUR
WHAT YOU WILL NEED

Setting up any business takes forethought. What you need will depend on the age of your students, the style of music you teach, where you teach and how much money you can spend to get started. You probably will not *need* everything listed in this section, but these items can make your teaching and business life easier. It is up to you to create a teaching environment that reflects who you are.

The three categories to think about when setting up your teaching business are office supplies, studio/teaching supplies and musical gear.

OFFICE SUPPLIES

COMPUTER AND PRINTER

You don't absolutely *have* to have a computer, but your business will probably run much smoother if you do. All your bookkeeping, scheduling, phone numbers and business correspondence will be safe in one location. You will need e-mail and internet capabilities. So much musical (and business) information can be found online that you will be working at quite a disadvantage if you are not using this vast resource.

OFFICE FURNITURE

This doesn't have to be anything fancy, but you will need a desk, a few chairs (especially if your office is also a reception and waiting area), lighting and a small table where you can stack magazines and other materials related to your studio. File cabinets come in handy to store hard copies of lessons, lesson policy and other business forms and records.

TELEPHONE/FAX MACHINE

The need for a phone is obvious, but having a fax machine can be pretty handy too. Most fax machines have a "copy" function as well. This can be useful when you need to make a small number of copies. Having a fax machine simply makes it easier for people to get in touch with you. Your lifelines are your phone, your fax machine and your e-mail account.

COPIER

These machines are expensive to buy or lease, but if you use a lot of handouts during your lessons, you will save time, hassle and money if you have one. You can keep your lesson masters on your computer or in a file cabinet and make copies as you need them. This is especially handy if the masters are hand written or not created on a computer. Having to go to a print shop to use their copiers takes time, and it's difficult to know exactly how many copies of a particular lesson you may need. With your own copier, you can simply make the copies you need.

CASH REGISTER/CREDIT CARD DEVICE

You'll be receiving cash, checks and credit cards. You want to make it easy for people to pay you for lessons. If you sell books, picks and strings, the need for these items is even greater.

OTHER NECESSITIES

You will also need paper, pencils, markers, pens, a stapler, tape, paper clips, calculator, pencil sharpener, stamps, envelopes, coffee maker(?), shelving or bookcases, receipt books, bulletin board, tacks and any other items that will help you run your office smoothly. It is also important to decorate your office. Paintings, posters and plants go a long way to "professionalize" your office space.

STUDIO/TEACHING SUPPLIES

TWO OR THREE CHAIRS

You will be spending a lot of time sitting down. Find a chair (armless, of course) that you *really* like. Good chairs can be expensive, but you'll save a lot of wear and tear on your body if you spend your teaching hours on a chair that is ergonomically correct.

Students come in all shapes and sizes. Be sure your student's chair is strong and comfortable. You may be surprised by how often you replace this seat. Also have a third chair in the room, as some parents like to occasionally watch a lesson.

MUSIC STANDS

One or two music stands should suffice if you are teaching one-on-one lessons. Obviously, more will be needed if you are teaching classes. While more expensive, the heavier metal stands are usually the best deal in the long run. Wire stands do not usually last very long, so they would have to be replaced more often. They also don't work very well with bigger, heavier music books.

FILE CABINET

If your office and teaching areas are separate, you'll probably want a second file cabinet. In the teaching area, you'll need access to lesson masters and other materials. File cabinets work well for this.

SHELVING/BOOKCASE

If you are like most guitar instructors, you probably own a ton of books, videos and other educational aids. Keeping them organized will help you find information faster. You also need a place for capos, slides, tuners, manuscript and TAB paper, picks and all the other little items we use to play and teach guitar.

COMPUTER

It's also helpful to have a computer in your studio. As a teaching aid, computers are hard to beat. You can:

- Create more professional looking handouts.

- Print copies as you need them.

- Keep records about what your students are currently working on.

- Create custom play-along tracks for individual students, quickly and easily.

- Demonstrate ideas and concepts with the help of backing tracks.

- Record examples, or even entire lessons, for your students.

- Download additional lessons and information from the internet.

- Use the computer as your primary listening device. CDs, MP3s and other music files are easily stored and accessed.

You will need software for standard music notation and TAB. Recording software is very helpful too. There are also ear training programs and programs that slow down recording speeds. This can be handy when transcribing lines and solos for students.

CD/MINIDISC/MP3 PLAYER

If you are not using a computer in your studio, be sure to have a CD player. You will need it to play recorded examples for your students.

Keep your recordings organized and easy to find so you don't waste lesson time. MP3 players make it very easy to organize recordings you use for teaching.

Some teachers encourage their students to record their lessons. If you provide the recording device, all your student has to do is bring a disk or cassette.

OTHER ITEMS

Good lighting is always important, so you will need to have the appropriate fixtures. Make it brighter than your reception area.

Sound-proofing may be an issue depending on where you are teaching. There are many ways to accomplish this, from expensive professional products—like acoustic tiles and baffles—to home-spun solutions such as hanging carpets and egg cartons, etc.

MUSICAL GEAR

Basically, you will need almost as many instruments as styles you can teach. It is important for a student to see you play an instrument that is similar to his/her own. There is nothing inherently wrong if this is not the case, but having the appropriate instrument makes you more credible to the student. Use a nylon-string guitar when teaching classical music, an electric guitar when teaching rock and a steel-string acoustic if that's what your student has. Set a good example for your students by keeping your own instruments clean and properly set up. Keeping a spare guitar around isn't a bad idea either. If a student's guitar self-destructs or becomes otherwise unplayable, he/she can still get through the lesson on the loaner.

AMPLIFIERS

If space or money is a problem, using a single amp might be necessary. However, if at all possible, have one amp for you and another for your student. Small amps of high quality are the way to go. Both you and your students sound better through great equipment.

DRUM MACHINE OR METRONOME

There are various times in a student's training when the use of a metronome is required. These work perfectly well, but working on time is a lot more fun for some students when they use a drum machine. While not a necessity, using one can make a student's lesson more enjoyable and memorable.

ADDITIONAL ITEMS

- Guitar cords—*lots* of them

- Strings

- Picks

- Capos

- Slides

- Nail files/buffers

- Tuners

- Polish

- Polish cloths

- String changing tools

- Allen wrenches

CHAPTER FIVE
THE BIZ

Performing and playing the guitar is fun. Teaching guitar can also be fun. When playing or teaching becomes your livelihood, you will probably have to start looking at some things a little differently. Don't worry, playing and teaching will still be fun, but remember that after you start your teaching business, you'll have to maintain it and work toward future goals as a teacher and business person.

So far we have concentrated on how to get your teaching business started. Now it's time to talk about *keeping* your business going strong. There may be some non-musical topics to think about. Not all your responsibilities will be great fun. However, if you put these ideas into place now and continue to follow through with them, your time will increasingly be spent on playing and teaching, and less on business administration.

ADVERTISING AND ATTRACTING STUDENTS

Students can come into your life from a variety of places. If you are primarily a working performer, audience members who admire your work may want to study with you. Some may want only a single lesson, while others choose to set up regular lessons. In either case, keep their contact information. This is important because it is challenging for performers who do not teach much to attract students. Clubs and concert gigs aren't always conducive to finding serious students.

If you teach in a music store, you will probably have no trouble signing up new students. This is because:

- People call or walk into the store inquiring about lessons.

- When customers buy a new guitar they often inquire about lessons.

- Your students will tell their friends about you.

- Your student's parents will tell *their* friends.

Word of mouth is by far the best way to acquire new students. Being professional and producing students that play well and with confidence are your best advertising.

Some music store owners spend a lot of time developing their teaching department because they know they are cultivating the sale of lots of strings, picks, instruments, etc. They actively advertise in the newspaper and telephone book to keep a flow of new students coming into the store. If this is the type of music store you teach at, consider yourself very lucky. In this situation you represent the store as well as yourself. Always conduct yourself accordingly.

If you are a new teacher at the store, offer to play a short concert for the students and the public. This will let people know you are affiliated with the store and looking for prospective students.

Fliers can also let prospective students know you are teaching in the area. After getting permission from the school, leave your information in the music department. Posting fliers in music stores and malls can also be effective. Be sure to call other teachers in the area and let them know you have some openings. They may have a few names to throw your way. Be sure to return that favor sometime in the future.

Running your own teaching studio will probably require you to advertise just like any other business. This means running ads in the Yellow Pages, newspapers and possibly even local radio. Advertising on the large screen at the local theatre is pretty effective as well. Advertising isn't cheap and you may have to try several methods before finding the one that works for you. Promoting your business at city events is another good way to let people know about you.

Still, word of mouth will be your greatest source of new students and this takes time to develop. There is a natural turnover in students every month and you should expect this. Some students simply lose interest. Others quit for financial reasons, or their swimming lessons and little league games get in the way. Whatever the reason, you always need to be on the lookout for new students. Decide how many students you are willing to take on and always try to maintain that number.

KEEPING STUDENT RECORDS

Right from the beginning with only a few students, you need to keep accurate records. Having good records can prevent embarrassing situations, like asking for payment when the student has already paid, or needing to reschedule a lesson only to find you've lost the student's phone number, or booking two (or more?) students in the same time slot. These situations can occasionally happen to even the most organized teachers, but if they occur too frequently your students will start to consider you as rather flakey and unreliable (and rightfully so). It's easy to keep this from happening. On pages 34 and 35 are two possible ways to set up your student records. Both are very easy. On page 34 is an example done on a computer (which can also be done in a spiral-bound notebook); on page 34 is an example using index cards.

"If you are a new teacher at the store, offer to play a short concert for the students and the public. This will let people know you are affiliated with the store and looking for prospective students."

In the example below, information about your schedule and students, on any given day, appears on a single page. At a glance you can see the lesson time, the student's name, phone number and payment record. You can add a space for "remarks" as well. Here you can make notes to yourself about what the student is working on, or other information you want to remember about this individual.

Student Record Sample—computer.

Student Records								
Monday Schedule			**Payment Status**					
Time	Student	Remarks	Jan	Feb	Mar	April	May	June
3:00 PM	Georgia Harrison (760) 555-1234	Working in Alfred Book 1, page 31	√	√				
3:30 PM	Rick Jagger (760) 555-4321	Villa Lobos piece, start 2nd part	√	√				
4:00 PM	Rodney Stewart (760) 555-1324	Needs to pay a week late	√					
4:30 PM	Maggie Mae (760) 555-2413	Jazz Guitar Harmony, page 13	√	√				
5:00 PM	Paula McCartney (760) 555-1423	Art of Solo Guitar, page 98	√	√				
5:30 PM	Jim Hendrickson (760) 555-2314	Owes for 2 months						
6:00 PM	Les Montgomery (760) 555-3214	Won't use a pick	√	√				
6:30 PM	Matt Patheny (760) 555-2431	Jazz Skills, page 42	√	√				
7:00 PM	Bill Holiday (760) 555-1432	Paid 3 months ahead	√	√	√			
7:30 PM	Gina Simmons (760) 555-2341	Beginning Blues, page 6	√	√				
8:00 PM	Edward Fitzgerald (760) 555-6987	Learning to sing and play	√	√				
8:30 PM	Paula Stammy (760) 555-6798	Beginning Jazz, page 22	√	√				

Student Record forms are included on the CD. There is a file for each day of the week—in Excel and PDF format. The Excel sheets are intended for those who prefer to keep their records on their computer. The PDF files can be easily printed so you can fill in your spreadsheets by hand. (Note: Adobe Acrobat Reader and Microsoft Excel are required to open these files.)

- Windows users can access these files by double-clicking on My Computer, then double-clicking on the CD drive icon.

- Mac users can access these files by double-clicking on the CD icon on the desktop.

Another way to stay organized is to devote a separate page or index card to each student. This allows more space for remarks, which can be handy when teaching more advanced students. Stack the cards (or pages) with the first student of the day on top. After that lesson, slip it underneath the stack and follow suit for each student. You will have a stack of cards for each day of the week that you teach. If a new student signs up, or one quits, it's easy to add or delete a card.

Student Record Sample—index cards.

3:00   MONDAY

DUKE WELLINGTON

PAYMENT RECORD: JAN, FEB, MARCH, APRIL
                     ✓   ✓

REMARKS: CURRENTLY WORKING ON MINOR SCALES
            FOR IMPROVISATION. NEEDS A BIGGER CHORD
            VOCABULARY. GOOD RIGHT-HAND TECHNIQUE.

4:30   TUESDAY

DIANE CRAWL

PAYMENT RECORD: JAN, FEB, MARCH, APRIL
                     ✓   ✓

REMARKS: PRIMARILY INTERESTED IN
            ACCOMPANIMENT STYLES FOR
            HER OWN VOCALS. GOOD STUDENT.
            LEARNS QUICKLY.

5:00   THURSDAY

JOHN SCOVILLE

PAYMENT RECORD: JAN, FEB, MARCH, APRIL
                     ✓   ✓   ✓

REMARKS: INTERESTED IN EFFECTS AND
            EQUIPMENT IN GENERAL.
            WORKING IN INT. JAZZ GUITAR,
            PAGE 99

BOOKKEEPING

Finding an easy way to keep track of your income and expenses will make your life much easier. You'll see how much money you are making and where that money goes. This will help you plan your business strategy. Your bookkeeping records tell you not only how much income it takes to keep your business running, but also whether or not you are spending too much in a certain area. At the end of the year, these records make figuring your taxes much easier.

Two tips to remember:

1. **Keep all receipts.** You'll need these if you ever need proof of your business expenses.

2. **Try to do your bookkeeping daily.** This isn't always easy to do, but if you wait too long to record your figures, mistakes are easier to make. If you are in the habit of taking care of your bookkeeping regularly, you won't have to go back as far in your records to find errors.

On page 37 is a sample chart for income and expenses. It is organized by month and divided into the categories, income and expenses.

INCOME

This section lists all teaching revenue. You can also include method of payment (for example, cash, check, etc.).

EXPENSES

- **Studio Rent**. This is a record of your studio rent payments. You could also list other overhead expenses, like electricity, gas, phone, etc.

- **Equipment**. Your equipment is a business expense. You can include anything from a new guitar to a capo or a pick. List it all.

- **Office Supplies**. Office supplies can be anything from paper clips to a new desk or lamp.

- **Miscellaneous.** Everything else falls in here. Your printing expenses, a book you need for reference, parking, postage, etc.

Of course your needs may vary from this list, but this is the general idea. If you do a lot of printing, for example, this could be a permanent column in your bookkeeping chart. After a while, you will appreciate the information you can glean from keeping your records accurate and up-to-date.

Income and Expenses

	January	February	March	April	May	June
Income						
Allen Ranch	$80.00	$80.00	$80.00	$80.00	$80.00	$80.00
Lois Lang	$80.00	$80.00	$80.00	$80.00	$80.00	$80.00
John Calzone	$160.00	$160.00	$80.00	$80.00	$80.00	$80.00
Patsy Kliner	$80.00	$80.00	$80.00	$80.00	$80.00	$80.00
Robert Bobber	$80.00	$160.00	$160.00	$160.00	$160.00	$160.00
Leslie Gorlick	$80.00	$80.00	$80.00	$80.00	$80.00	$80.00
Kenneth Gee	$80.00	$80.00	$80.00	$80.00	$80.00	$80.00
Peter Moss	$160.00	$80.00	$80.00	$80.00	$80.00	$80.00
Michael Smith	$80.00	$80.00	$80.00	$80.00	$160.00	$160.00
Susan Bright	$80.00	$80.00	$80.00	$80.00	$80.00	$80.00
Randy Streets	$80.00	$160.00	$160.00	$160.00	$160.00	$160.00
Bob Daisy	$80.00	$80.00	$80.00	$80.00	$80.00	$80.00
Don Lemon	$80.00	$80.00	$80.00	$160.00	$160.00	$160.00
Mitch Jaggar	$80.00	$80.00	$80.00	$80.00	$80.00	$80.00
Patrick Edward	$160.00	$160.00	$160.00	$160.00	$160.00	$160.00
Joanie Styles	$80.00	$80.00	$80.00	$80.00	$80.00	$80.00
April May	$80.00	$80.00	$80.00	$80.00	$80.00	$80.00
Josh Martinez	$160.00	$160.00	$80.00	$80.00	$80.00	$80.00
Rufus Brion	$160.00	$160.00	$160.00	$160.00	$160.00	$160.00
Tiffany Jewel	$80.00	$80.00	$80.00	$80.00	$80.00	$80.00
Sarah Smile	$80.00	$80.00	$80.00	$80.00	$80.00	$80.00
Tony Ian	$80.00	$80.00	$80.00	$80.00	$80.00	$80.00
Jimmy Pager	$80.00	$160.00	$160.00	$160.00	$160.00	$160.00
Nancy Bilson	$80.00	$80.00	$80.00	$80.00	$80.00	$80.00
Sebastian Backer	$160.00	$160.00	$160.00	$160.00	$160.00	$160.00
Emily Haines	$80.00	$80.00	$80.00	$80.00	$80.00	$80.00
Jimi Camaro	$80.00	$80.00	$80.00	$80.00	$80.00	$80.00
William Bosby	$80.00	$80.00	$80.00	$80.00	$80.00	$80.00
Total Revenue	$2,720.00	$2,880.00	$2,720.00	$2,800.00	$2,880.00	$2,880.00

	January	February	March	April	May	June
Expenses						
Studio Rent	$150.00	$150.00	$150.00	$150.00	$150.00	$150.00
Equipment	$12.00	$23.95		$75.00		$12.00
Office Supplies	$4.75	$15.00	$175.00			$3.75
Miscellaneous			$6.00		$60.00	
Total Expenses	$166.75	$188.95	$331.00	$225.00	$210.00	$165.75

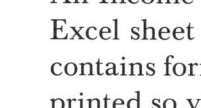

An Income and Expenses form is included on the CD—in Excel and PDF format. The Excel sheet is intended for those who prefer to keep their records on their computer; it contains formulas you can use to keep track of your finances. The PDF files can be easily printed so you can fill in your spreadsheets by hand. (Note: Adobe Acrobat Reader and Microsoft Excel are required to open the files.)

- Windows users can access these files by double-clicking on My Computer, then double-clicking on the CD drive icon.
- Mac users can access these files by double-clicking on the CD icon on the desktop.

PROMOTION

Coming up with ideas to promote your teaching business is fairly easy, but executing your plans can be quite time consuming. The time you spend promoting your business is usually well spent. Here are some ideas to help you get started.

Idea: Play a concert at your studio (or music store).

Work involved

- Getting a group together.
- Paying the group.
- Advertising/fliers, etc.
- Seating.
- Noise considerations?

Idea: Student Recital.

Work involved

- Preparing each student. This can mean extra sessions with your students, maybe even a recital rehearsal.
- Advertising/fliers, etc. Friends and relatives will be more than willing to attend, so they need to know about it.
- Seating.
- Noise?
- Refreshments?

Idea: Special Clinics and Seminars.

Work Involved

- Inviting a guest teacher to teach his/her specialty.
- Teaching the clinic yourself. Choose a topic with wide appeal, or something more specialized.
- Creating and printing handouts and other materials you may need.
- Seating?
- Noise?

Idea: Monthly Newsletter.

Work Involved

- You'll need computer time and the skills to create your newsletter. This is not difficult—it just takes time to learn the software.
- Figuring and planning your postage costs.
- Creating and developing content. Articles? Lessons? Contests?
- Keeping your database of recipients up-to-date.

Idea: A Teaching Website.

This can be a place for students to check out information about you and your business. You can offer lessons, contact information and even explanations of your curriculum and teaching philosophy. If you're really ambitious you can list your students' weekly assignments there.

Work Involved

- Creating and maintaining the website.

- Making regular updates.

- If you plan to sell products from your site, you will probably have to pay for server space. Your domain name in this case will also have a cost. If you do not plan to sell products, there is a lot of free space out there but you'll have to use the name the host company gives you.

- Websites tend to generate a lot of e-mail. You'll need time to respond.

SELLING BOOKS, CDS AND OTHER SUPPLIES

We've touched on this topic earlier but here is some additional information to help you decide if you want to sell items at your studio. There is a big difference between a teaching studio and a music store. If you want to open a music store, you should have plenty of general business experience and perhaps even a business degree. Don't be intimidated, though. It is very manageable to stock and sell a few items that are related to your teaching business.

Let's assume you will only sell items that relate directly to your teaching. For example: strings, picks, books and CDs you use to teach with, and perhaps accessories like slides, capos and tuners.

Before you open your teaching business you will probably need to register a business name and fill out some forms. This will vary from city to city and state to state. Don't worry, it isn't difficult and the people who work in city hall are there to guide you through the paperwork.

You will also need to know your state's laws regarding sales tax and other fees that might be required.

Other responsibilities that go with selling products at your studio include:

- Tracking and maintaining inventory.
- Orders and returns.
- Making sales.
- Creating and maintaining your studio's display area.
- Additional bookkeeping.
- Dealing with manufacturers and, possibly, sales people.
- Shopping around for the best deals.

All this may sound complicated but once it is all set up—and you have some experience making it work—you can get back to your real job, which is teaching of course.

ATTENDANCE AND CANCELLATION POLICIES

In most cases, your students will look forward to their lessons and wouldn't think of not showing up without calling you. Still, you need to have an attendance/cancellation policy in writing so there are no misunderstandings. Your students have certain expectations of you, and they need to know you have a few expectations of your own. Here are some ideas to think about:

- **Be sure your students know that you do expect regular attendance.** Everyone misses a lesson now and then, but chronic no-shows tie up valuable time slots and end up costing you money. If you have students like this, simply suggest that taking lessons at this time might not be a good idea and they are welcome to come back when a stronger commitment can be made.

- **Your students should know that you do expect to be paid on time.** You shouldn't have to beg for your money. If you charge by the month, a friendly reminder one week before the payment is due will help keep your fees coming in on time. Charging monthly helps to ensure attendance. Some teachers will make up lessons as long as the students cancel 24 hours in advance. Other teachers are so busy they can't do make-ups at all. If a student misses a lesson, they are simply out the money. If you try to charge for each lesson individually your money will sort of "dribble" in all month. If students don't show up, you'll never be paid for your time. Charging monthly gives you a clearer picture of how much you are actually earning.

- **Make sure your students know you expect them to practice.** You do have to be reasonable here. You will find some students are very serious about their lessons. Others may not be at all. Most will fall somewhere in between so you need to be fair about your expectations. If a student misses a few days of practice now and then, it's really no big deal. If they rarely practice, then you need to have "the talk." Once again, suggest that this might not be a good time for them to commit to lessons, and you hope to hear from them some time in the future. Some progress has to be made each week, or lessons quickly become a waste of your time and the student's time and money. If you are reasonably satisfied with a student's progress, then that student is practicing enough. All students have their own practice issues and you must deal with each one individually.

"Your students have certain expectations of you, and they
need to know you have a few expectations of your own."

GENERATING ADDITIONAL INCOME

If you are running your own teaching studio, here are some ways you can generate more cash flow.

- **Rent your studio space to local bands that need a place to practice.** Most teaching studios are only open when lessons are going on. The rest of the time the place is closed. Some businesses charge an hourly rate for rehearsal space. Some charge in three-hour blocks. You might be able to rent space to several bands on a regular basis and bring in a noticeable increase of income.

- **Present concerts and charge admission.** You can play yourself or bring in guest artists.

- **Conduct clinics or special classes and charge a fee.** It could be a single three-hour class or an ongoing class that runs for several weeks.

- **Create a band program as an additional part of your teaching business.** You could offer a band experience for beginners as well as more advanced students. Each band could have a regular practice time each week at your studio. You get the bands together and help them rehearse, and arrange for performances every now and then. Your charge for this program would be based on how many hours per week you devote to it. You may need additional equipment for this, but you can make that money back by renting equipment to others when it is not in use.

- **Offer your studio to other teachers to use.** If you have no students on a particular day, why not let another teacher rent the space from you? Depending on how big of an operation you want, you could take on quite a few additional teachers and collect studio rent from all of them.

"You could offer a band experience for beginners as well as more advanced students. Your charge for this program would be based on how many hours per week you devote to it."

CHAPTER SIX
BASIC TEACHING CHOPS

In a way, teaching is a lot like being on stage. You talk, play, tell an occasional joke or story and all the while you are diagnosing your student's playing, increasing his/her musical understanding and just being a positive, encouraging human being. Teachers juggle many skills and like most other endeavors, experience will be *your* best teacher. Here are some things to think about.

PERSONALITY

We are all human and subject to our ups and downs, but in professional situations we must never sink below a certain level. In general, being optimistic and enthusiastic will help your student feel more comfortable during a lesson. Some students may feel pretty vulnerable. They get embarrassed about mistakes or feel silly when "On Top of Old Smokey" is played badly. Your confident and glowing personality helps them get through these moments. Always be reassuring and let them know that time and practice will take care of most problems.

THE FIRST LESSON

When a student shows up to the first lesson, you want to take care of a few practical matters. First, confirm that the day and time of the lesson is going to work for them.

Then go over your attendance and cancellation policy, the payment policy and what you expect in terms of practice. Be very friendly, but also serious about all of this. You are setting the tone for the business aspects of your relationship with this student.

The next thing is to inspect the student's guitar. Check the intonation, setup and general condition of the instrument, and make casual suggestions about how to fix any possible problems. Even if the instrument needs a lot of work, try to find something positive to say about it. After all, everyone loves their guitar.

Next, show them the books and other materials they'll be using. This is also a good time to mention other items they may need, like a music stand, footstool or strap. You aren't really trying to sell them anything. You're just being helpful by telling them what they will need over time.

SIZING UP YOUR STUDENT

You must know a little about a person before you can effectively teach them anything. Certain things, like approximate age, are obvious. You and your student are going to get to know each other fairly well over time. It's perfectly all right to ask about their family, occupation and other interests they may have. This isn't being nosy. This information will help you teach this individual on a higher level. When you can teach someone in terms they can relate to, you are being the ultimate teacher. Getting to know your students personally will make you a better teacher.

Ask about earlier musical experiences. Did they ever take piano lessons? Trumpet lessons? What sparked their interest in the guitar? What are their goals? A casual player? Serious amateur? Part-time pro? Pro?

Look at them and look at their guitar. Is the instrument too big for them? Is it too small? Is the string gauge correct for their size and strength? Are there injuries or irregularities to their hands?

You should also look for more serious things, too. Does this student seem to have a short attention span? Is there any indication of a learning disability? Is this person under the influence? Does he/she seem stable? Usually everything turns out fine, but remember that anyone can call and sign up for lessons. Just keep your eyes open for potential issues.

TEACHING DIFFERENT AGE GROUPS

YOUNG CHILDREN

It is entirely up to you to define the boundaries of your business. Some teachers work only with adults and teenagers, and some specialize in working with younger children. If you decide to instruct younger kids, say ages 7 through 12, it may be a good idea to keep the following in mind.

Remember that young kids have shorter attention spans. With some you may find it difficult to hold their attention for a full half hour. This is a major consideration when deciding to work with students this young. You will need imagination to come up with ways to hold their interest. There are many good books and CDs for very young guitar students. With a little research you should be able to find musical games and toys that could help you teach as well. Using practice charts and rewards, like stickers or even guitar picks, can be good motivators. In particularly challenging situations where the child just can't sit still, invite the parent to sit in on the lesson. Sometimes this helps. Kids mature at different rates so you may have an 8 year old who does fine and a 10 year old that can't sit still. Expect that some kids will take lessons, then quit, only to sign up again. This could go on for some time before he or she "takes" to it.

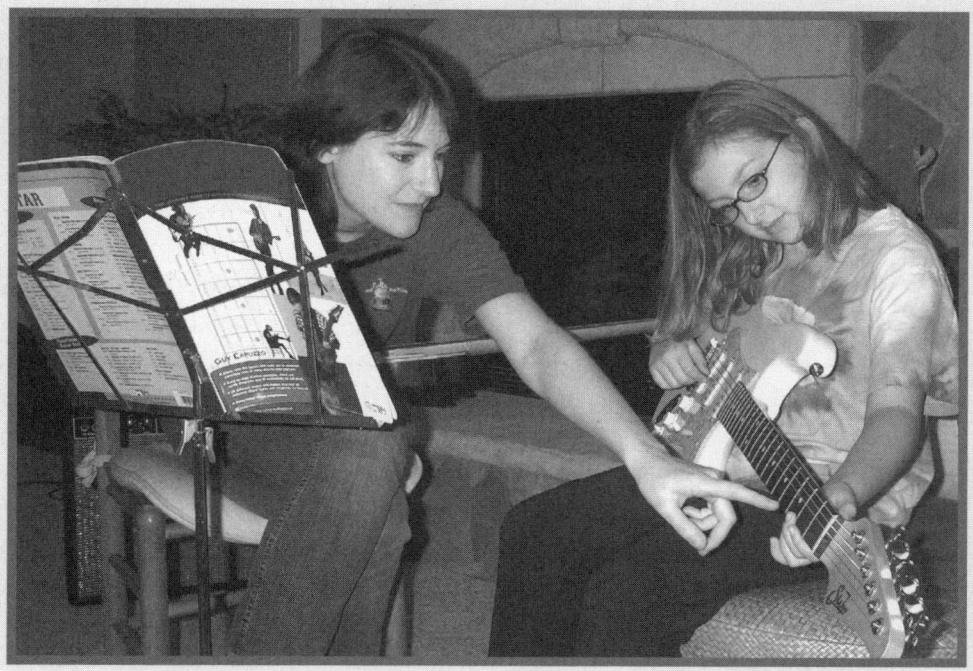

"You will need imagination to come up with ways to hold [children's] interest. There are many good books and CDs for very young guitar students. With a little research you should be able to find musical games and toys that could help you teach as well."

TEENAGERS

If you are going to work with teenagers, it is probably a good idea to know their world, at least musically. While you will have students who may want to learn classical music or jazz, your teen students will most likely want to learn the pop music they listen to. If you like and listen to the same music, all should go well. Always be open, however, to learning all kinds of music to expand your range as a teacher. You should be able to teach guitar "basics," like reading, technique and fretboard knowledge, to almost anyone. When it comes to style-specific information, however, you have to know the groups, songs and techniques of the genre. You can't fake it, either. Teenagers have pretty good radar for that sort of thing.

Many students in this age group have a pretty good idea of what they want to learn. This is fine, but it is up to you to make sure they are also learning the things they *need* to know as well. This can take diplomacy. Always explain to your students *why* they are working on certain things that seemingly have little to do with what they want to play. You have the overview—let them in on it.

If you are simply showing songs, or parts of songs, to your students, you really are not teaching. You must teach the instrument itself, and general musical concepts, along with styles and songs. As examples of theoretical ideas you are teaching, use songs your students like. Teens think their music is cool. It's your job to teach it to them while showing that the theory and technique behind the music is also cool.

If you are close in age to your teenage students you need to maintain your teacher's authority. You'll seem a little cooler to them, but you have to make sure they still take you seriously.

ADULTS

Many adults study guitar as a hobby, and quite a few are very serious students. They generally know what they want to study and why. For many, learning guitar is a way to expand their lives beyond work and family.

Adults usually know "how" to learn, especially if they have been relatively successful in other areas of their lives. Most adult students, it seems, used to play in younger days and are interested in getting back to it. They will be interested primarily in classic rock, blues and jazz. Three issues are common when teaching adults:

1. **You may be much younger than some of your adult students.** Some may find this awkward. As long as you maintain a professional demeanor, there should be no problem. If you are doing your job well, and the student still has a problem with this, suggest an older teacher that you may know. It's the student's issue. No blame.

2. **Adult students, although well meaning, do not usually have much practice time.** They will show up feeling badly about this. Just encourage them and possibly assign a little less each week for a while. Assigning a long-range project is another good way around this situation. Tell your student to master only the first eight measures of their assignment this week. Next week, take the next eight bars and so on. While progress is slower, successfully reaching their weekly goal is much more likely.

3. **Sometimes adult students who are quite successful in their careers have a problem when they don't immediately succeed in their guitar studies.** It's up to you to let them know that there is a real learning curve involved and it may take longer than they think to master what they are working on. Some adult students just aren't used to being beginners again. Try to keep these lessons fun, but remember that they do still want a challenge.

UNDER-TEACHING

Most inexperienced teachers are a little surprised by this concept, while more seasoned teachers know it well. In the beginning, many instructors tend to give too much information or assign too many things to practice. Often, this is because they want to give the students their money's worth. Most of the time, however, it's because they have forgotten how long it took *themselves* to absorb some of this material. After many years of teaching and playing, we develop an overview of the guitar and music in general. With this perspective we tend to see how all the information "fits" together. Most of your students will probably not have this overview. To them, the new concepts and techniques are not yet interconnected and take longer to learn. You need to remember this. What may seem like an average size assignment to you, may seem like a mountain of work to your student. Always under-teach. Your student should *easily* reach his/her goals each week. You want your students to succeed each week. They will feel better about you, their lessons and their own progress. It may take a few lessons to find a student's threshold for work. Play it safe by under-teaching.

TEACHING GOOD PRACTICE HABITS

The question inevitably comes from every student: "How should I practice?" Or, "How can I get more out of my practice time?"

There are many ways these questions can be answered. It really depends on your own personal views and the student's level of ability. The following ideas are an overview of this subject and are generally considered sound. Use them as a point of departure to develop your individual philosophy.

- Practicing a little every day is better than practicing for very long periods once or twice a week.

- Warming up for a few moments before practice will make your practice session more productive.

- Some educators believe you should practice one thing at a time until it is mastered. This improves your performance in other areas as well.

- Other educators believe you should divide your time into smaller segments, working on a variety of things.

- There are basically two types of practice: 1) Learning and applying new ideas (conceptual practice), and 2) Physical (motor skills) practice. Some teachers suggest that the best use of daily practice time is for learning new skills and material. Television time can be used to maintain your motor skills by running through scales, arpeggios and other exercises.

- Electric guitar students should always practice with their amps. The amp is part of the instrument.

- Beginners need about half an hour of daily practice. Young kids may need their parents' help.

- All others should practice *at least* a half hour per day. If you are alert and paying attention, more practice leads to faster progress in most areas.

DEALING WITH DIFFICULT STUDENTS

This is pretty much a no-brainer. Adult students who are disruptive or extraordinarily disagreeable should be dismissed immediately. The behavior of younger students and teenagers is the responsibility of the parents. Do not be afraid to call parents if you need to. After the parents' initial embarrassment, they will usually do what they can to help you. You are not a babysitter. If a student doesn't want to learn or be there, he/she is wasting the time slot and ultimately costing you money.

ENCOURAGEMENT AND CRITICISM

This falls under the category of "people skills." You have to be sensitive to your student's feelings and still get your points across. It's very easy to see (or hear) what is wrong with a student's playing. It's also very easy to dwell on these things until your student's self-esteem plummets. When addressing a problem with a student's performance, try to also point out something they are doing well—even if it's a very small thing. You could say things like, "I really liked how you played this section. Your timing was very good and your picking sounded nice and even. I think your left-hand fingering needs a little work, so let's concentrate on that for a while. Let them hear the good things first. They will be more receptive to criticism after that. Don't sugar coat—be honest but sensitive. Tell them how long it took *you* to learn certain things.

DIAGNOSTICS: TARGETING A STUDENT'S DIFFICULTIES

The ability to pinpoint a student's difficulties and problems is probably the most important skill a good teacher has to develop. While very general, the points below should help you get to the bottom of many problems students may have.

- Check the student's posture. This affects everything the student plays.

- How is the guitar positioned? Some beginners tend to lay the guitar flat on their laps. Others hold the neck out in front of themselves.

- Check left-hand position. Sometimes a change in wrist or thumb position can remedy many things.

- Check left-hand fingering. Is the student using the fingertips? Pads? Are the fingertips placed well? Is there enough pressure being applied? Too much?

- Check the right-hand position. Is the wrist being held accurately? What about pick position and technique? Are dynamics being observed?

- Does the student understand the meaning of everything on the printed page?

- Does the student understand the concepts behind the assignment?

- Is the student trying to play too fast?

- Is the student practicing too fast? Practicing enough?

- Does the student have insecurities that inhibit his/her performance?

A mental checklist like this eventually becomes automatic as your diagnostic skills improve. Once again, try to balance all your criticisms with positive comments.

CHAPTER SEVEN
BASIC INSTRUCTIONS FOR ALL STYLES

The following basics should all be taught, regardless of curriculum for individual musical styles: posture, holding the guitar, using a strap, left-hand position and fingering, basic pick-style technique, basic fingerstyle technique, reading notation, reading TAB and tuning.

POSTURE

- **Emphasize the importance of good posture.** Every part of your body works better when your spine is straight. Coordination is better too.

- **Explain how consistency in posture leads to consistency in playing.** Good playing posture should become a consistent habit. Where and how you sit matters as well. If you practice while sitting on the floor one day, on the bed the next day, a straight-back chair the following day and standing up the day after that, you can't expect consistent progress, especially in the beginning. Try to practice in the same chair every day.

HOLDING THE GUITAR

- **Classical style, with footstool.** The guitar rests on the left thigh. The left foot rests on the adjustable footstool.

- **Resting on the right thigh.** Most electric and acoustic steel-string players prefer this position.

- **Holding the guitar upright and close.** It is important to emphasize this because many students tend to tilt the face of the guitar slightly upward, adversely affecting their left-hand position. Some even go so far as to lay the guitar on their laps, strings facing upward. This should be corrected.

- **Good neck position.** Some beginning students hold the neck of the guitar out in front of them. Have them pull the neck inward, so it is right under their nose when they look to the left.

USING A STRAP

- **Why use a strap?** Explain how holding on to the guitar with your arms and hands can diminish your playing skill. Let the strap hold the guitar for you so your hands are completely free to play.

- **Adjusting the strap.** The higher you wear your guitar the more control you will have. Adjust the strap so the guitar rests against you in the same spot, whether you are standing or sitting. Once again, consistency is important here.

LEFT-HAND POSITION AND FINGERING

- **Thumb position.** Keep the left thumb behind the neck in "hitchhiking" position, pointed away from you. The thumb can wrap around the neck for leverage if you are bending a string. Otherwise, try to keep the thumb in back.

- **Wrist position.** Keeping the left wrist straight facilitates free and more nimble finger movements. Try not to let your wrist bend too much in any direction.

- **Keeping fingernails short.** Keep the nails of the left hand short enough so they don't strike the surface of the fretboard. You want to play with the fingertips. If the nails are too long, the student's fingers will tend to "angle in" on the strings instead of landing directly down on them.

- **Placing fingers directly behind (just to the left of) the fret wires.** This will ensure proper intonation. It also takes less pressure to sound a note if the string is held firmly against the fret.

- **Using fingertips only.** Playing with the fingertips promotes better accuracy and nimbleness.

BASIC PICK-STYLE TECHNIQUE

- **Holding the pick.** Encourage your student to use a standard size pick—nothing too gimmicky.

- **Open strums.** Show basic strumming technique using open strings. Stress the importance of good wrist movement. Strive to make upstrums sound the same as downstrums, in terms of volume and tone.

- **Picking single notes.** Show how to play downstrokes by letting the pick come to rest on the adjacent string. Once this is achieved consistently, the student should practice this on all strings. Later, have the student match the sound of their downstrokes with upstrokes. An excellent exercise is to have the student spend two minutes per string, per day, matching the sound of their upstrokes and downstrokes.

BASIC FINGERSTYLE TECHNIQUE

- **Right-hand position.** Talk about hand position and keeping the wrist elevated. Show how you can assign various string sets to different fingers. Practice striking strings with rest strokes (with various finger combinations) until the sound is consistent.

- **Explanation of fingering designation:** thumb=*p*, index=*i*, middle=*m*, ring=*a*, pinky=*c*.

- **Nail care.** Keep this simple in the beginning. Just talk about length and buffing out the nicks.

READING STANDARD MUSIC NOTATION

- **Why learn to read?** Explain that being able to read standard music notation will help them learn and understand new material faster, and contribute to their becoming a complete musician. Stress literacy.

- **Methods.** There are good reading methods for beginning, intermediate and advanced guitar students. Some teachers insist that their students complete at least a basic reading method.

- **Supplemental reading.** Books with classical studies for clarinet, violin, flute and saxophone are great to use as additional reading material for guitar students.

- **Tips.** Tell your students to keep their eyes moving along at all times when reading. If they look back in the music to see if they played something wrong, they will probably lose the time or start making mistakes. Also, tell them to try to read ahead so their fingers are more prepared for what's coming. Reading music becomes a lot like reading text when you keep these ideas in mind.

READING TAB

- **Why read TAB?** Be honest here. TAB can make certain things easier to learn and can clarify fingerings, but it is not preferable to reading standard music notation. Players of bowed string and non-string instruments do not use TAB. Why should we?

- **How to read TAB.** This is easily explained with diagrams you can make. Instructions for reading TAB are also found in many method books.

TUNING OPTIONS

- **Tuning by ear.** It's usually a good idea to start here first. Relative tuning at the 5th fret (4th fret for the 3rd string) is easy to teach. Tuning by ear develops a certain intimacy with your guitar. This also reinforces other skills the student will need later on, like when ear training.

- **Using a pitch pipe.** You don't see these around much anymore, but they can be useful to help the student match pitches.

- **Using an electronic tuner.** There is no question that this is the most common way of tuning. Your student eventually needs to learn how to use one. They should learn to tune by ear first, though.

CHAPTER EIGHT
TEACHING FOLK GUITAR

A NOTE ABOUT CHAPTERS EIGHT–ELEVEN

If you've been teaching guitar for a while, you know that teaching style evolves over time. Most teachers choose to use their own methods along with other materials to provide a well-rounded curriculum. In time, most instructors put together a good program that works for them.

If you are just starting to teach, you will probably find these last four chapters very useful. There is no standard curriculum for teaching guitar that everyone agrees on, and there is no World Council of Guitarists to decide these things. This means we have to find our own way.

The sample curriculums in these chapters are exactly that—*samples*. After getting the basic ideas, you can adopt the parts that work for you. Since various styles of music require different teaching techniques, every style has its own chapter. In each, you will find a curriculum outlined, with comments and/or examples of lessons that could be used. Remember that this is only a very general guide to be used as a starting point.

When a student comes to you for folk guitar lessons, they are primarily interested in learning to play songs. They most likely want to accompany themselves singing. While they are learning some of the fundamentals from the last section, it is a good idea to start introducing open position chords and other basic chords. Show them chords that are related to each other by key. This way they can start learning songs right from the start.

LEARNING BASIC CHORDS

Since most folk songs are rather simple harmonically, learning the chords most frequently used in common keys is a logical place to begin. The chords most commonly used in folk music are the I chord, the vi chord, the IV chord and the V7 chord. By learning these chords and having a basic introduction to scale and chord theory, the student could learn many songs and even be able transpose them if necessary. The following examples show these chords in some of the more common keys for folk songs. They are shown with chord diagrams, standard music notation and TAB. It's a good idea for students to be comfortable with all three methods.

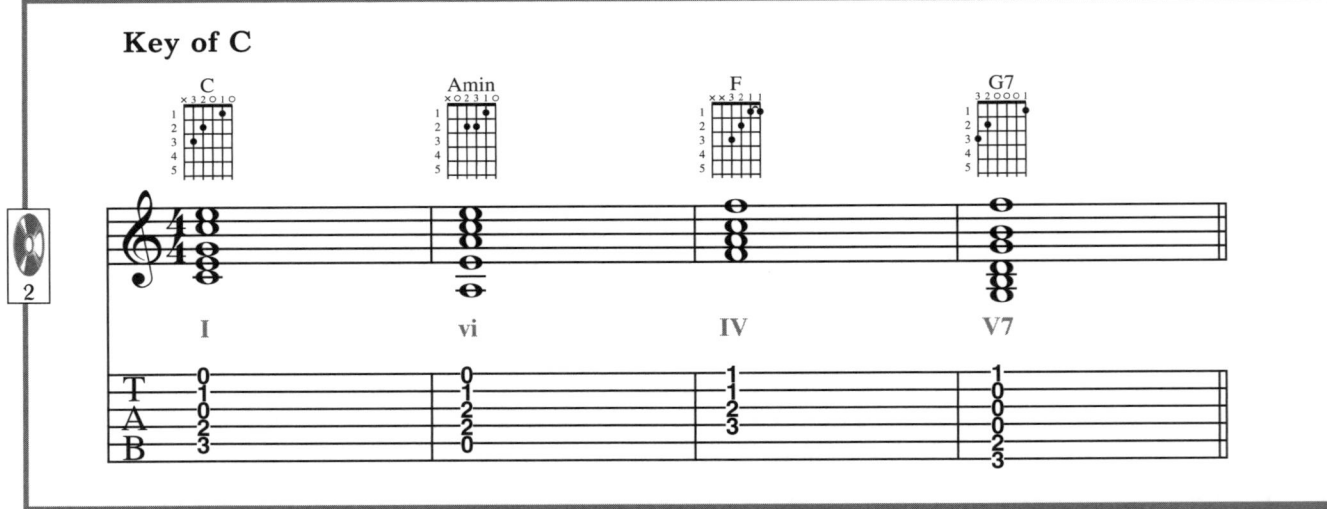

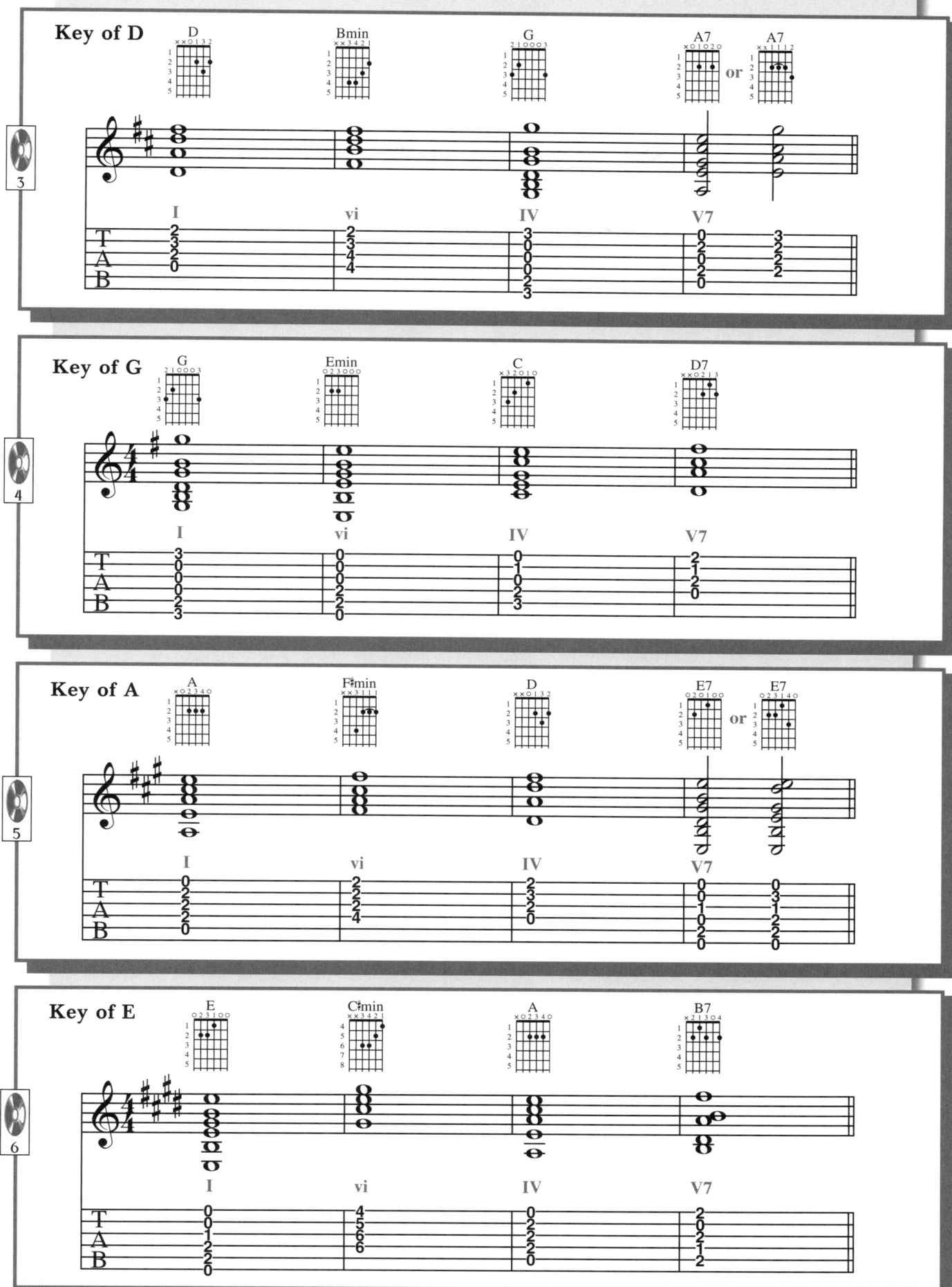

Be sure to mention that the fingertips may get a little sore for a while. If your students have difficulty with stretches or partial barres, tell them to stretch into the chord (or hold down the barre) for about 30 seconds, and repeat this over and over again. This will accelerate their progress. They will see more results through stretching and holding than by just forming the chord and letting go right away.

STRUMMING PATTERNS AND CHORD CHANGES

The next thing you want to show your beginning folk student is some strumming patterns with a pick. Start with easy patterns that use all downstrums. Gradually introduce upstrums and more complicated patterns. Work on counting and keeping the tempos steady.

One problem most beginning guitar students encounter is changing chords in time. Many times the student will start a chord change extra early to get to the next chord in time. Tell them they should only play the song as fast as they can *accurately* make their chord changes. Slowing down and speeding up throughout a song is not a habit you want them to get into. This will be more difficult to correct later, so take care of it right from the beginning.

One way to help a student learn to make smooth chord changes is to dissect the move finger-by-finger to see *exactly* what is involved. For instance, when changing from a basic D Major chord to an A7 chord, point out that the 1st and 2nd fingers on the D chord keep the same basic shape when moving to the A7 chord. They each simply move over one string. Little tips like this go a long way. Next, you might have the student strum the D chord and let it ring for a full four beats, then change to A7 and hold that for a full four beats. When your student can do this successfully, have him/her hold each chord for only two beats. Then try one beat each and—if possible—try playing them as eighth notes.

"The next thing you want to show your beginning folk student is some strumming patterns with a pick. Start with easy patterns that use all downstrums."

Here are some strumming patterns using the basic chords shown previously.

FINGERPICKING

After your student can strum a few patterns and change chords in time, you can introduce fingerpicking. You'll need to address the following issues:

- **Hand and wrist position.** Beginners usually want to rest their right wrists on the bridge or saddle of the guitar. Remind your student to elevate their wrist instead.

- **Thumb** *(p)* **and 1st finger** *(i)* **"collisions."** For some reason, when this occurs students will sometimes pluck outward instead of holding the hand in place. These *p* and *i* collisions can be avoided by placing the thumb closer to the neck and swinging the remaining fingers back toward the bridge.

- **Make sure all strings can be played at the same volume.** It is easy to play louder with the thumb than the rest of the fingers, and you don't want the melody or other important parts of the fingerpicking pattern to be "drowned out."

- **Projection.** Train your student to play with power at first. You can work with a variety of dynamics later.

- **Comfort.** Most beginners working on fingerpicking find the overall hand position uncomfortable at first. Reassure them they will get used to it quickly. Eventually it will feel quite natural.

Start off with easy patterns like these below. Suggested left-hand fingerings are provided under the TAB.

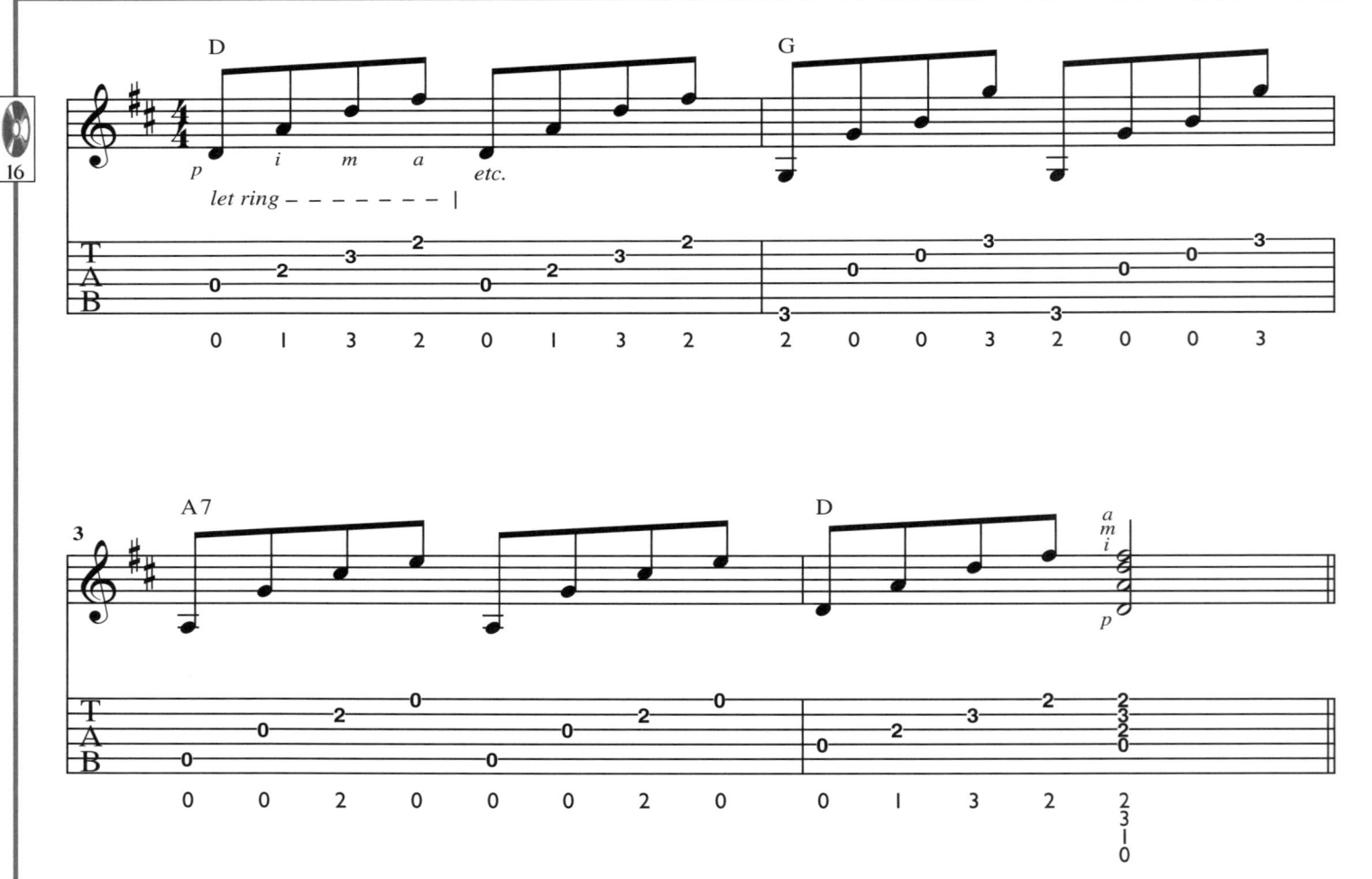

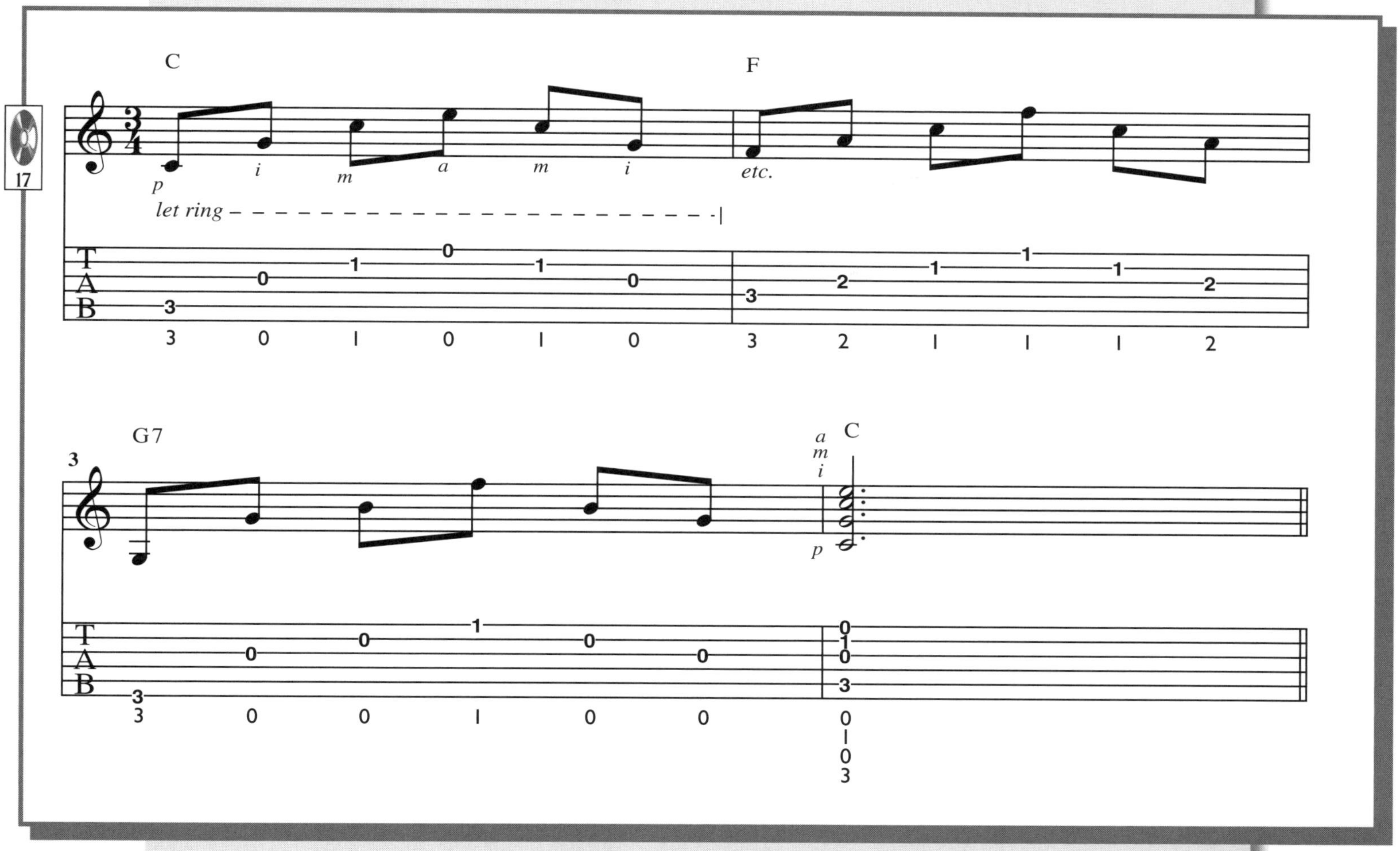
17
C
F
p i m a m i
etc.
let ring
G7
C
a m i
p
T A B

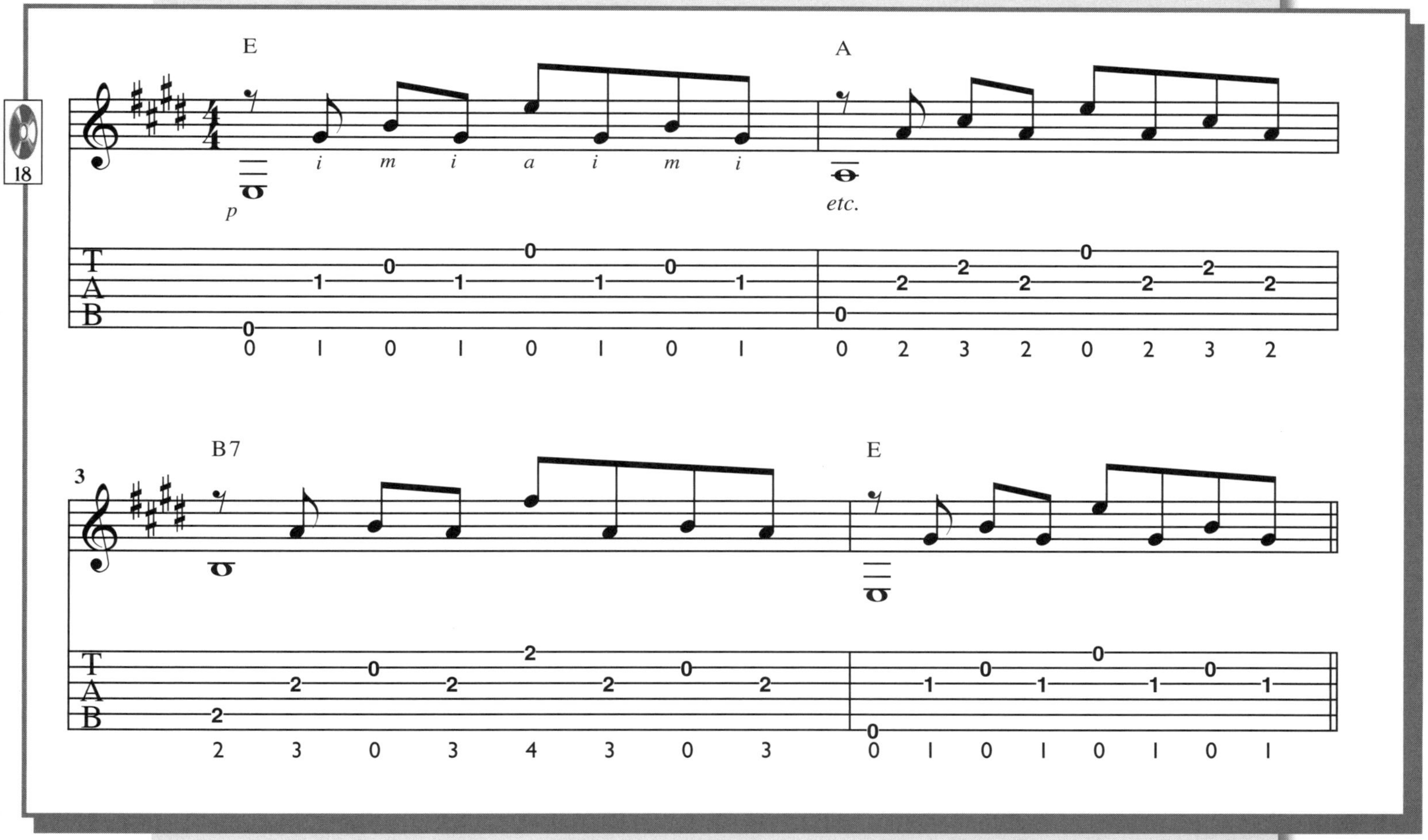
18
E
A
p i m i a i m i
etc.
B7
E
T A B

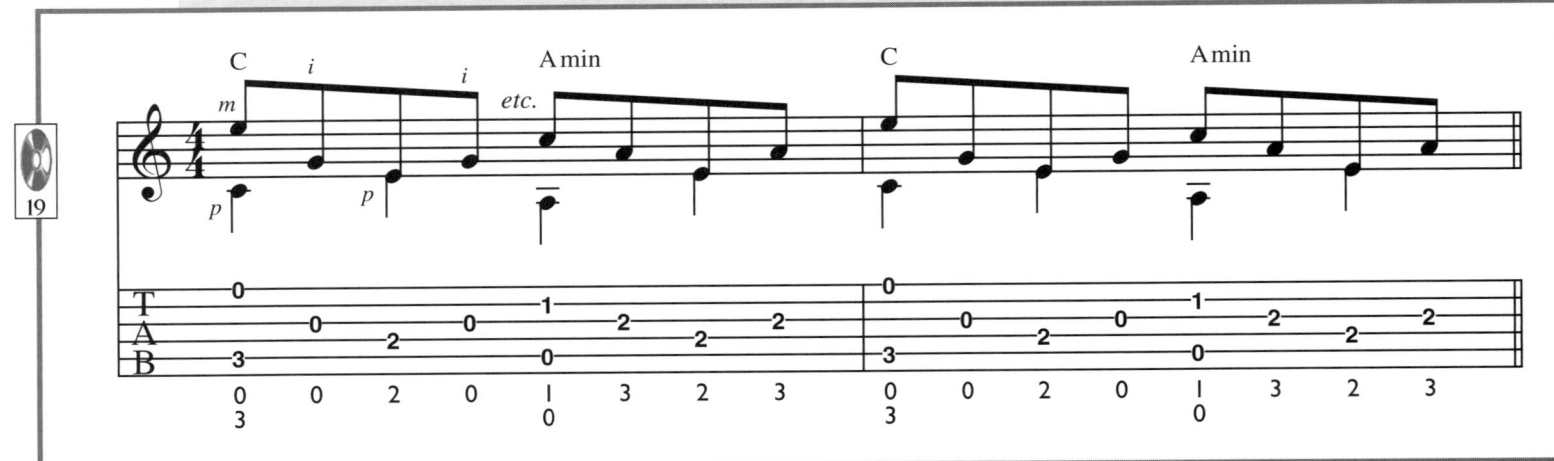

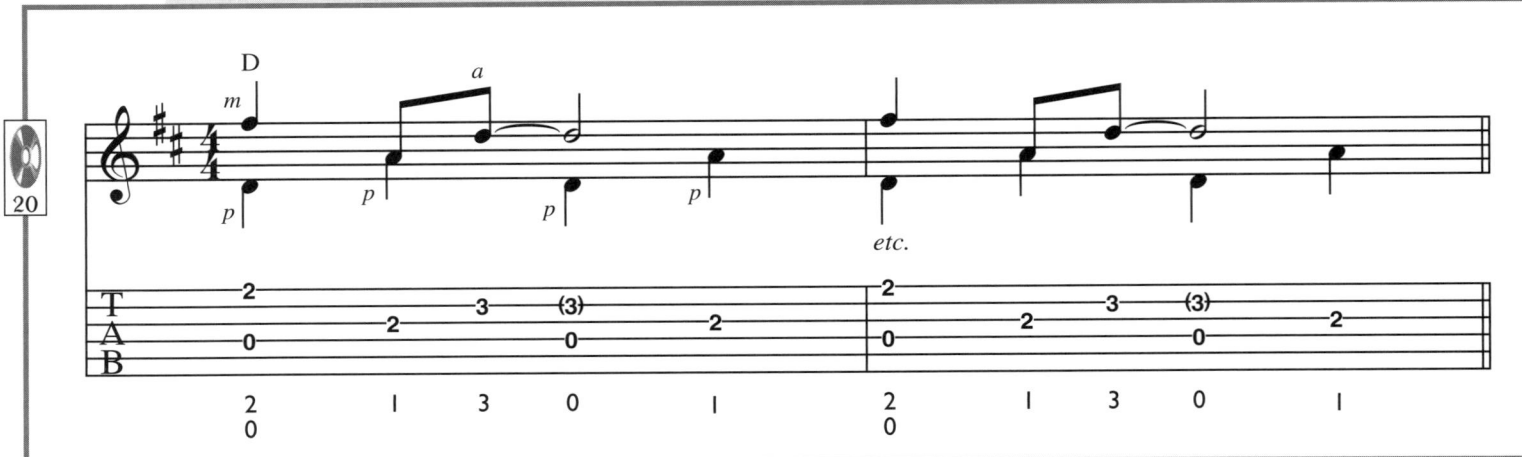

Of course, all these chords and strumming and fingerpicking patterns do not mean much unless you give the students songs to play. Every time you introduce a new chord, pattern or bit of information, your student should be assigned songs over many weeks that reinforce the new skill.

Other topics your folk students should be exposed to include:

- Using a capo

- Alternate tunings

- Bass runs and fills

- Instrumental "breaks"

Be sure to recommend folk artists they should listen to. This will encourage questions from your students, as well as inspire them and widen their view of the folk guitar world.

CHAPTER NINE
TEACHING BLUES GUITAR

A *lot* of people love the blues, so there is a good chance your student roster will include more than a few aspiring blues players. Working on the blues will introduce a student to many different guitar skills, such as playing various rhythms, learning scales, improvising, bending notes and coaxing the "right" sounds from their equipment. After your student has acquired the fundamental skills mentioned earlier, he/she may be ready to take on some blues studies. Even though there are many "styles" of blues, the basic tools we have to work with in each are remarkably similar. Of course, when it comes to technique alone, blues played on an acoustic guitar can require very different physical skills than blues played on an electric guitar. The following information can be used as an overview and starting point. These suggestions should help you organize your own methodology.

BARRE CHORDS

We all remember how difficult it was to learn our first barre chords, and just when we mastered one, our teacher would show us another. Instead of surprising your students with these chords, it may be a good idea to give them an overview of most of the common barre chords used in the blues all at once. This doesn't mean they have to learn to play them all at the same time, just learn how they are organized. Over time they can work little-by-little on each one until they have learned them all. Tell them they are about to learn two different sets of barre chords: those with roots on the 6th string (bottom of page) and those with roots on the 5th (page 59).

ROOT-6 BARRE CHORDS

Below are some root-6 barre chord shapes commonly used in the blues. The hollow dots indicate chord roots.

○ = Chord roots

Major	Minor	Dominant 7th	Dominant 7th
1 3 4 2 1 1	1 3 4 1 1 1	1 3 1 2 1 1	1 3 1 2 4 1

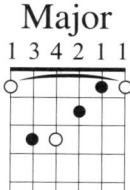 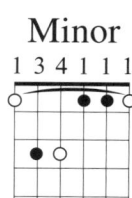  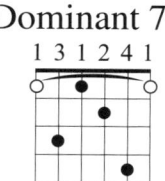

Below left is a diagram of the 6th string. By moving the chord shapes on page 57 up and down the neck, we can travel from root to root. For example:

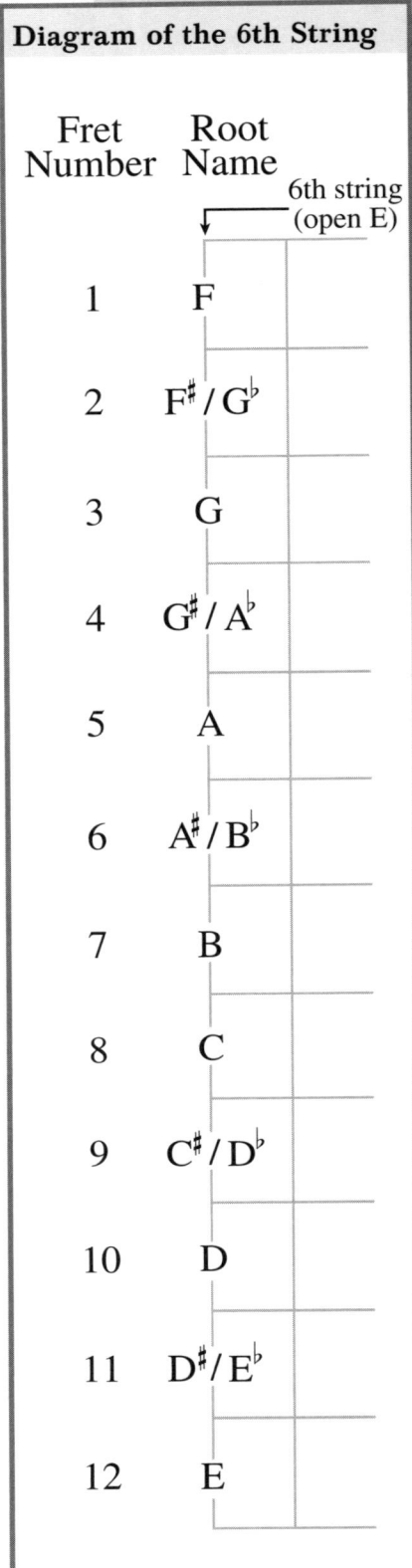

Diagram of the 6th String

Fret Number	Root Name	6th string (open E)
1	F	
2	F♯/G♭	
3	G	
4	G♯/A♭	
5	A	
6	A♯/B♭	
7	B	
8	C	
9	C♯/D♭	
10	D	
11	D♯/E♭	
12	E	

Playing a major shape at the 3rd fret produces a G Major barre chord, which is referred to as "G."

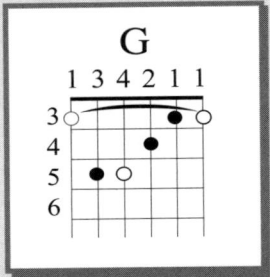

Playing a minor shape at the 5th fret gives us an A Minor barre chord.

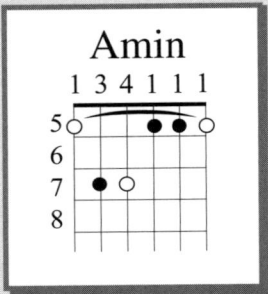

Playing a dominant 7th shape at the 8th fret produces a C7 barre chord.

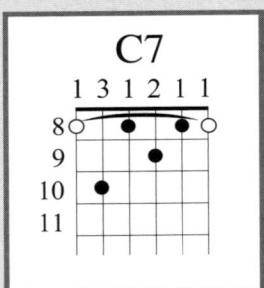

And so on.

ROOT-5 BARRE CHORDS

Here are a few root-5 barre chord shapes commonly used in the blues.

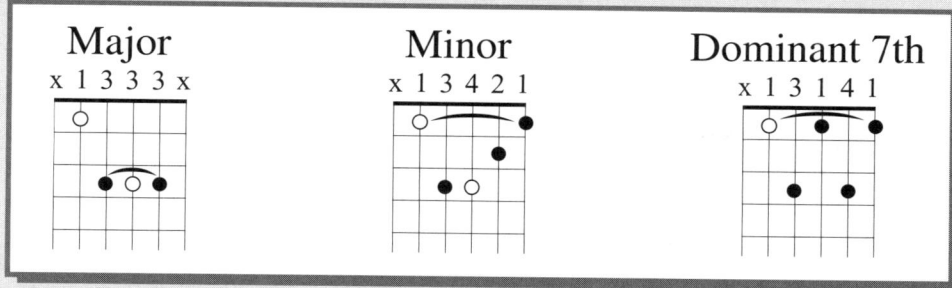

Below left is a diagram of the 5th string. Once again, by moving the above chord shapes up and down the neck, we can travel from root to root.

Diagram of the 5th String

Fret Number	Root Name
5th string (open A)	
1	A♯ / B♭
2	B
3	C
4	C♯ / D♭
5	D
6	D♯/ E♭
7	E
8	F
9	F♯ / G♭
10	G
11	G♯ / A♭
12	A

Playing a major shape at the 3rd fret produces a C Major barre chord.

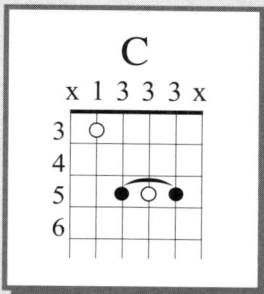

Playing a minor shape at the 5th fret produces a D Minor barre chord.

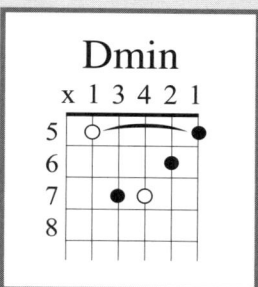

Playing a dominant 7th shape at the 8th fret produces an F7 barre chord.

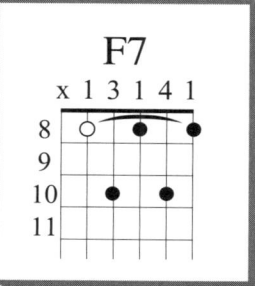

EXERCISES FOR MEMORIZING BARRE CHORDS

The following exercise can be used as a template to help students learn all moveable chords. You can have a student play this using all major, minor or dominant 7th chords, from either or both sets (root-6 or root-5). As your student learns new moveable shapes, assign a progression like this to help him/her assimilate the new information.

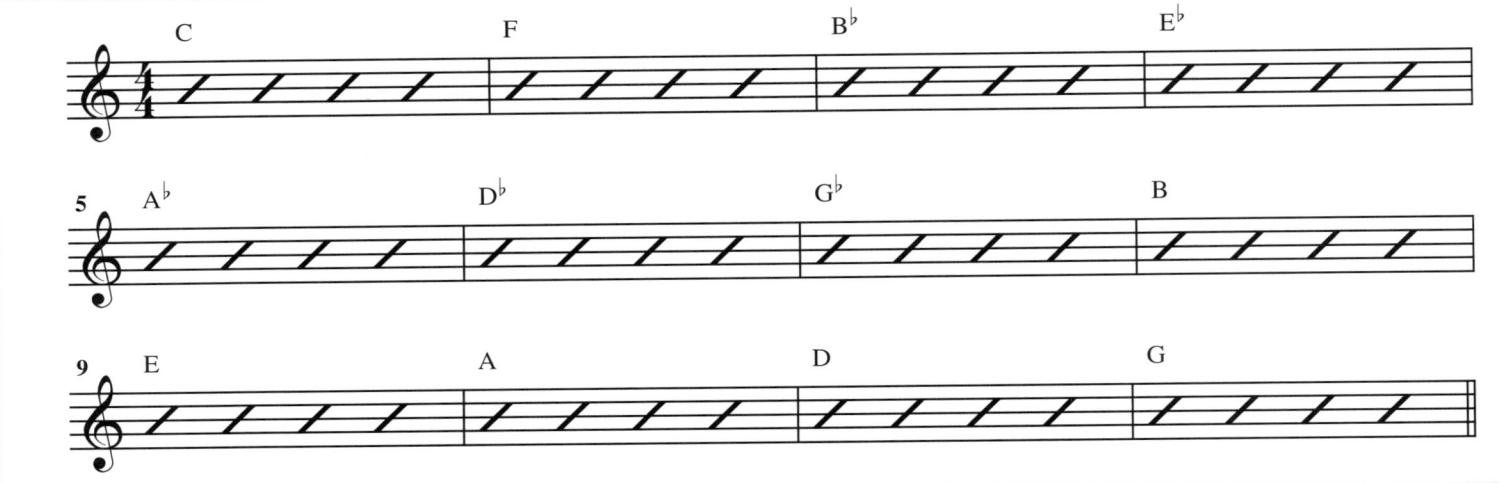

9TH CHORDS

9th chords are just as common in the blues as major, minor and dominant 7th chords. Explain to your student that they are often used as substitutes for the dominant 7th chords they have been learning. Encourage them to experiment with this. The above practice progression could be used again with all dominant 9th chords. Below are three 9th chord shapes.

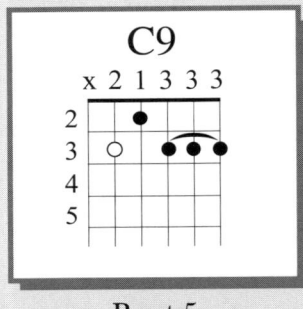

Root 5

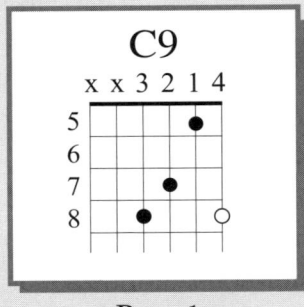

Root 1

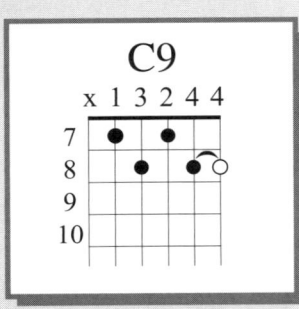

Root 1

THE BLUES PROGRESSION

It is usually necessary to define the term "blues" for your students. The word "blues" is used for so many different things a new student may not understand that it is, from a theoretical perspective, a musical form. Be sure to mention that the blues is a 12-measure musical form based on three chords. Even when there appears to be many chords, they are still usually based on the same three chords. If your student has had some theory training, you may want to explain how the blues progression is based on the I, IV and V chords. Later, go on to explain the function of diminished chords and secondary dominants in the blues form. If they're not quite ready for this info, start them off playing some simple blues progressions, and gradually begin discussing the theoretical aspects of the blues. Theory is assimilated more easily when applied to something the student is actually working on.

MAJOR BLUES PROGRESSION

It is probably best to start a student off with the Basic Major Blues Progression shown below. Both this and the Common Major Blues Variations that follow are in the key of A. However, you should have your students go through them in a number of different keys. Don't forget to inform them that in the blues, any chord can be turned into a dominant 7th (or 9th) for more of a bluesy sound.

BASIC MAJOR BLUES PROGRESSION

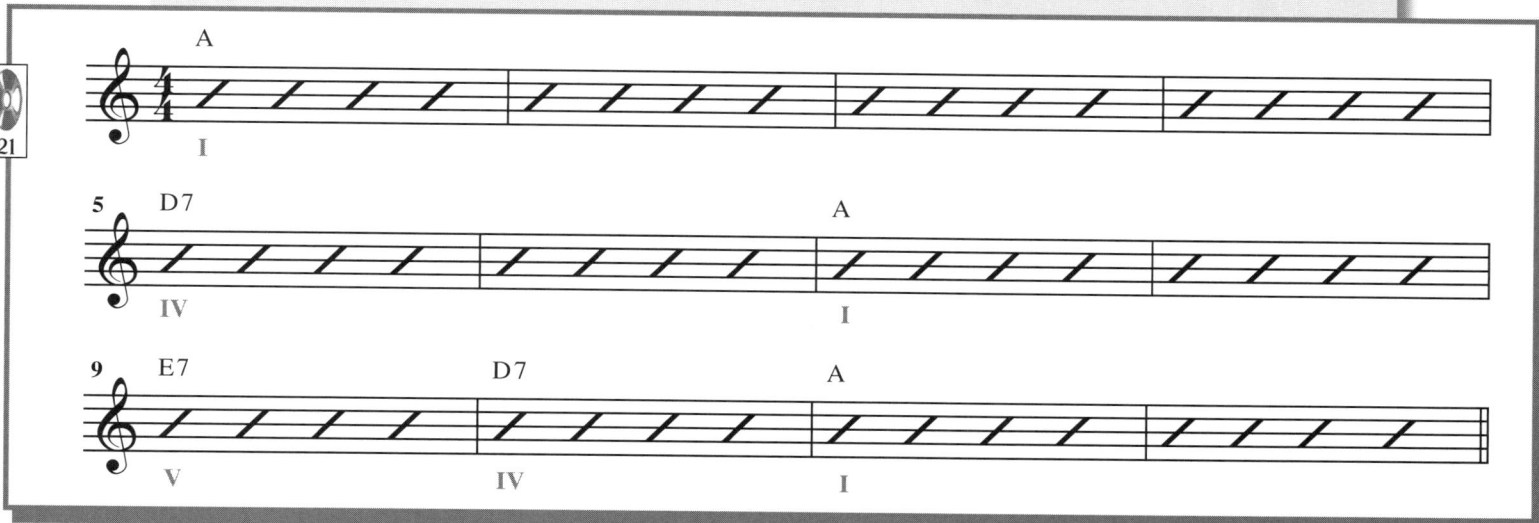

COMMON MAJOR BLUES VARIATIONS

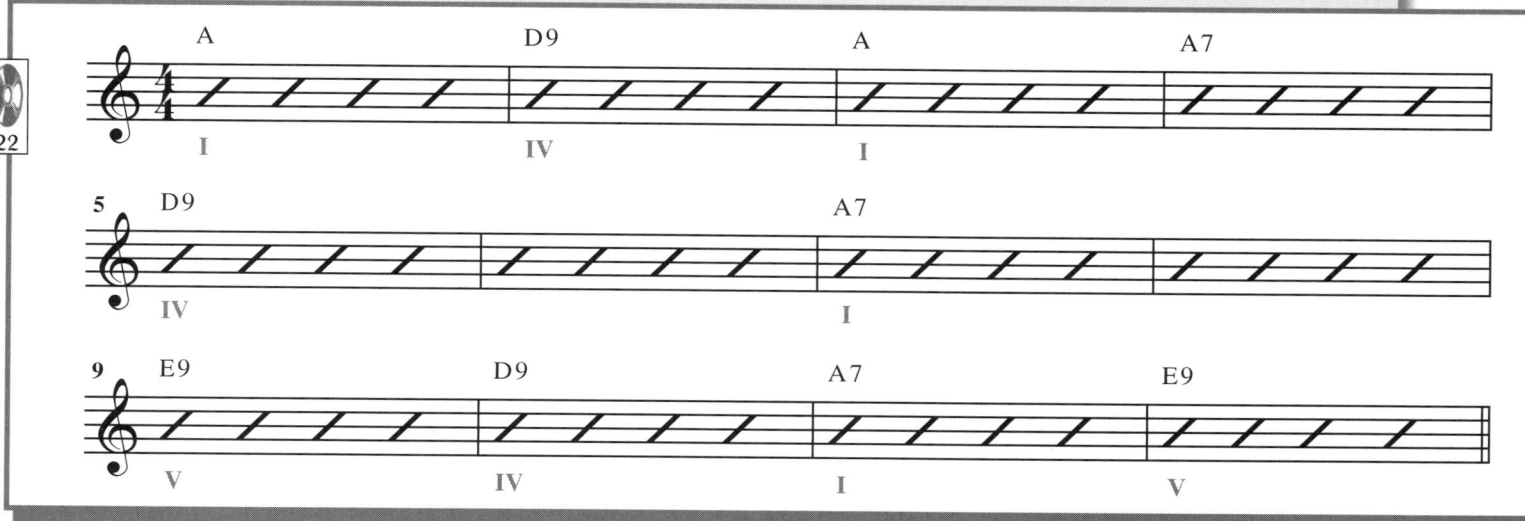

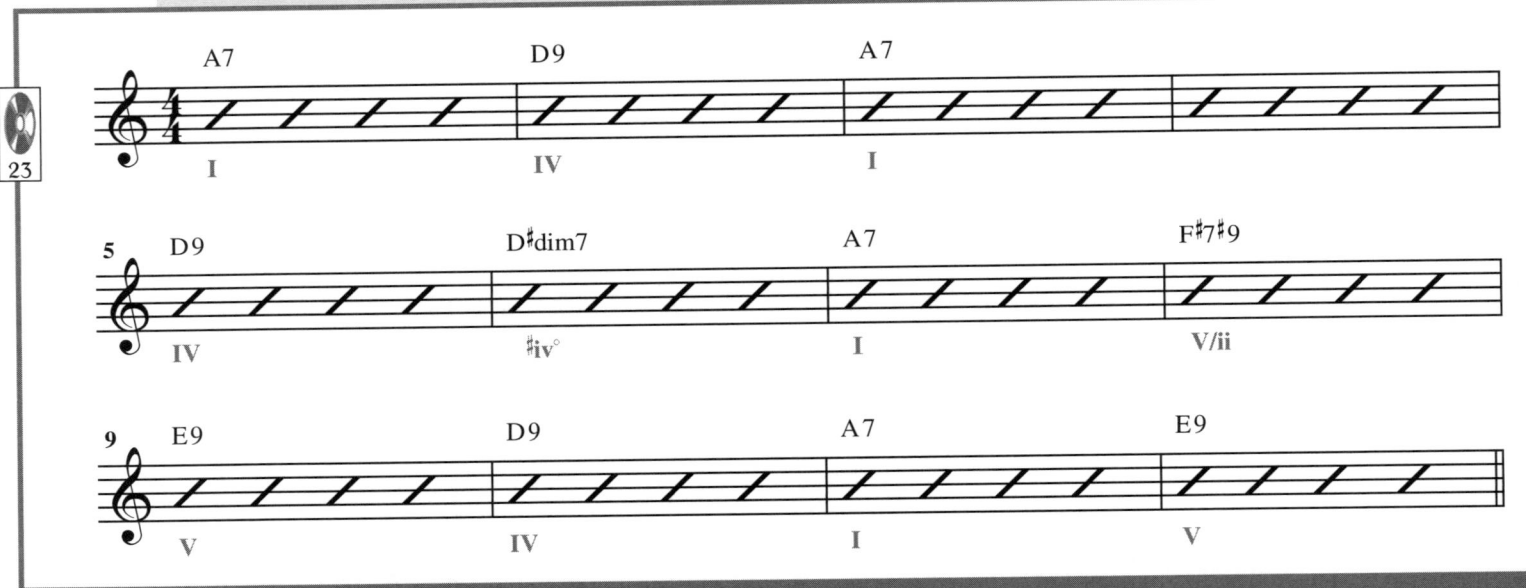

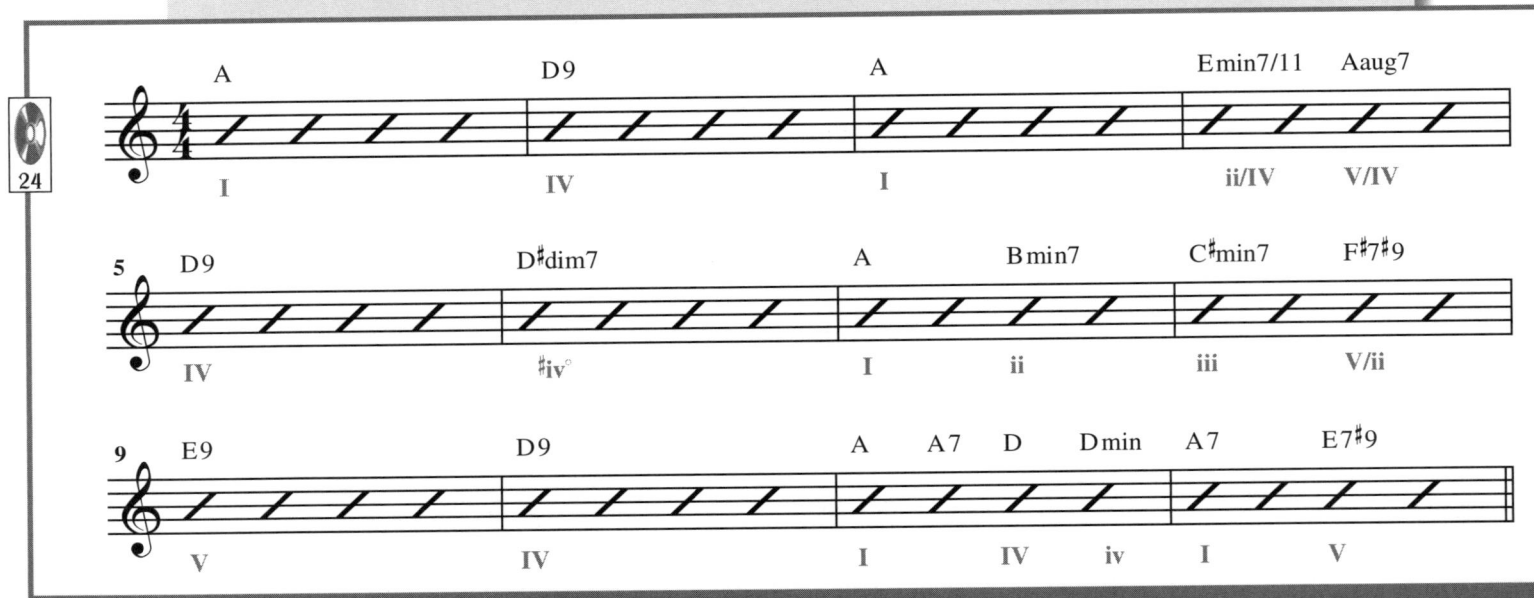

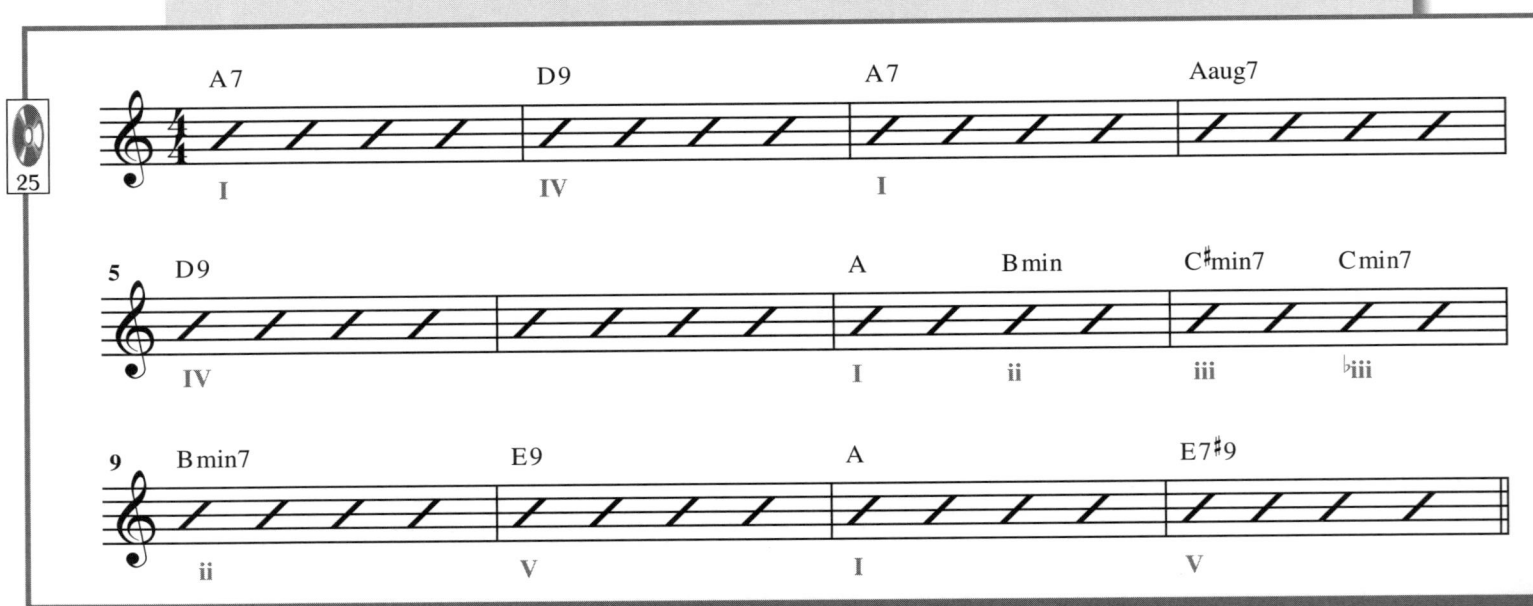

MINOR BLUES PROGRESSIONS

After some time working on major blues progressions, most students enjoy learning blues progressions in minor keys. Like the major blues examples, we start with the most basic progression and introduce variations later. Have your students learn them all in a number of different keys.

BASIC MINOR BLUES PROGRESSION

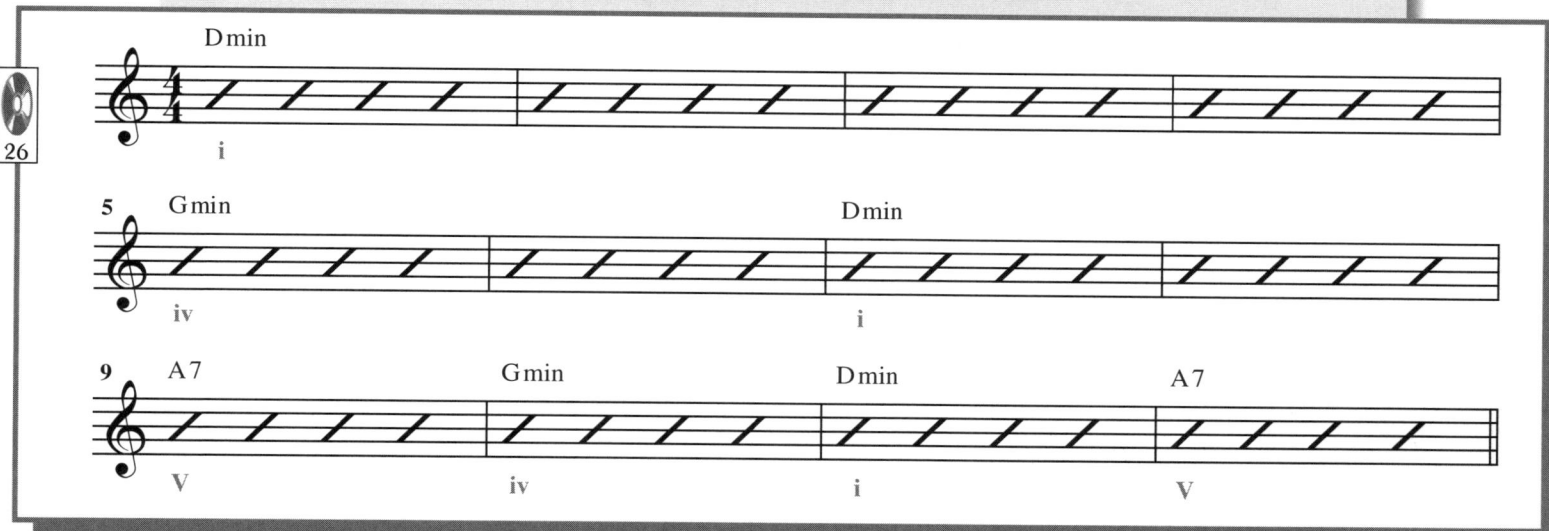

COMMON MINOR BLUES VARIATIONS

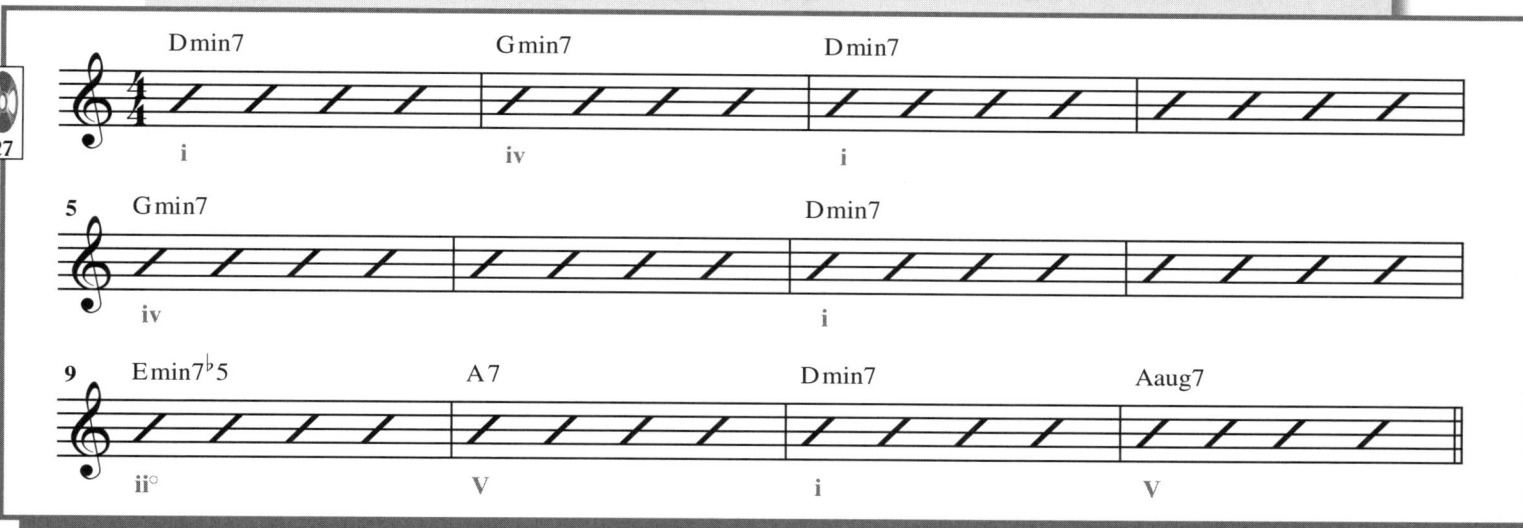

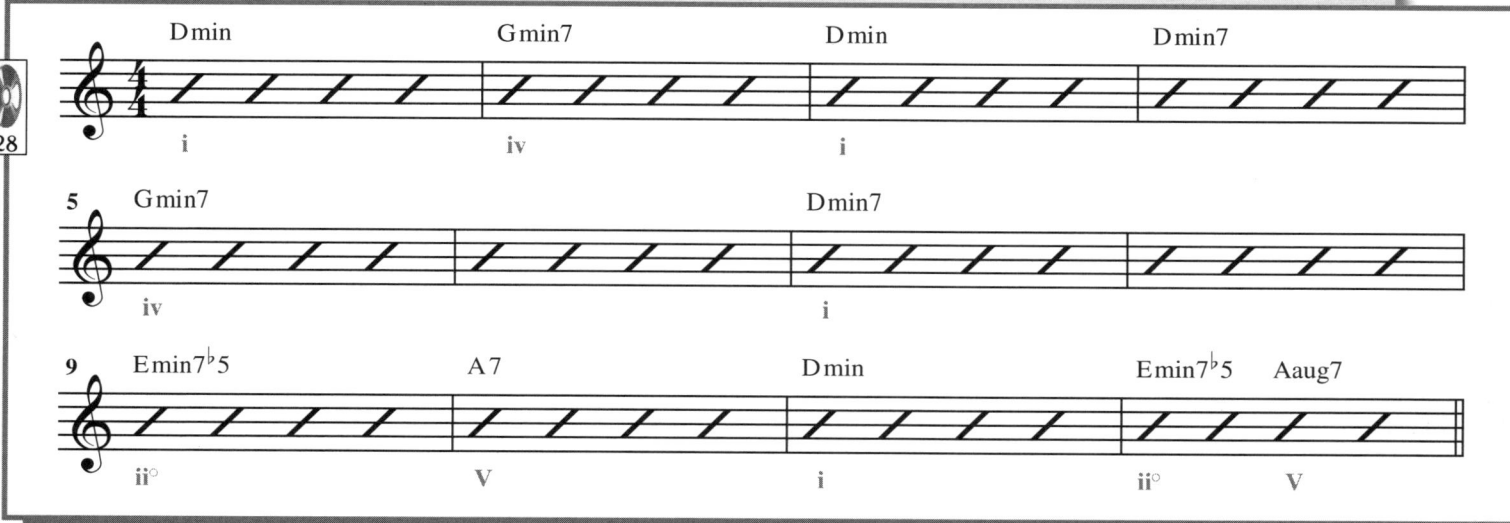

BLUES RHYTHMS

The rhythms used in blues music are some of the most readily identifiable. Slow blues, shuffle blues and rhythms using straight eighth notes should all be addressed with your blues students. Keeping a steady tempo is one musical value that should be talked about frequently. A steady tempo from beginning to the end is the goal. Have your students explore dynamics while they're working on these rhythms. Also explain the difference between "straight" eighth notes and "shuffle" or "swing" eighth notes (two eighth notes played like a quarter note and an eighth note in triplet rhythm ♩ ♪). In this book, swing rhythm is indicated at the beginning of a piece of music with: *Swing 8ths*.

The following rhythms are common and should be among the first they learn. There are countless variations. A solid foundation on the examples below will help your students learn the endless variations that exist in the blues world.

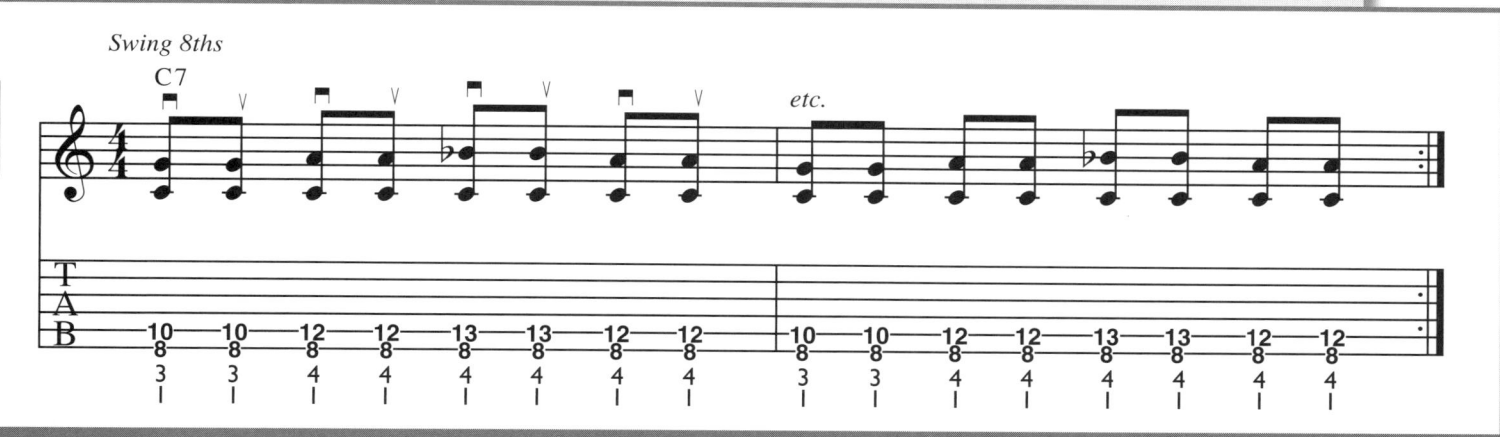

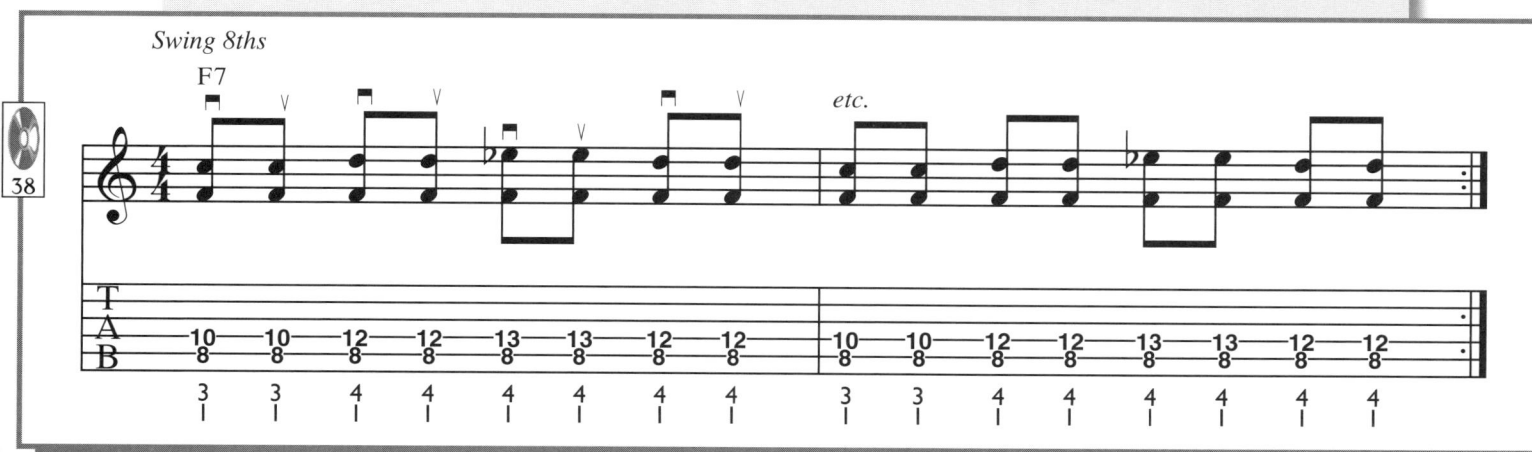

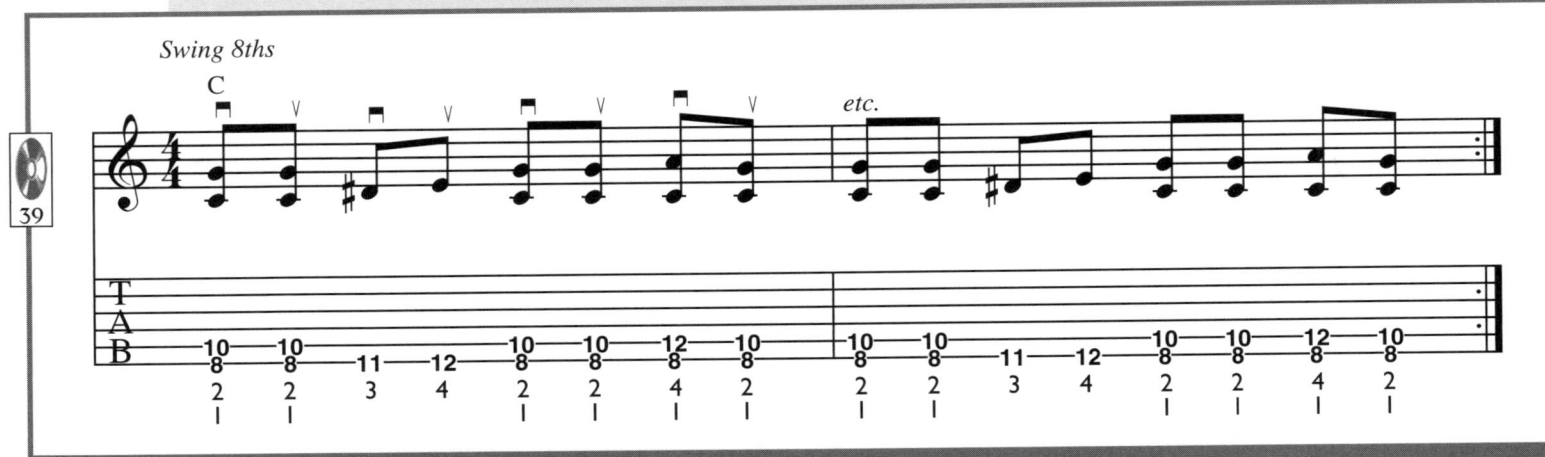

SCALES FOR BLUES

This is where the fun begins for many students. Many players that improvise in other styles often had their first experiences with the blues. The three most common scales to use for blues improvising are the minor pentatonic scale, major pentatonic scale and the blues scale. It is not necessary to give your student this overview just yet. Work with one scale at a time. Have the student memorize the fingering first. Then as he or she starts to play the scale ascending and descending, check to make sure their technique is correct and all the notes are being played at the same volume. This is important. Whatever the student gets used to hearing is perceived as correct. Uneven picking, unchecked, can be quite a nasty habit to correct later on. Teach dynamically-even picking right from the start.

You will find *many* fingerings for the common scales that follow. Remember that all the examples given are merely suggestions. Everyone has fingerings they favor. For your student's sake, stress consistency in whatever fingerings you show them.

MINOR PENTATONIC SCALES

Minor pentatonic scales are good first fingerings to show your blues students because they are easy to learn and have a familiar sound to most people. If your students listen to a lot of blues, they will find themselves able to copy some of the blues vocabulary almost right away. Below are some suggested fingerings. Make sure to have your students go through them in a number of keys. The gray dots indicate the tonic notes of the scale.

C MINOR PENTATONIC SCALE FORMS

⬤ = Tonic

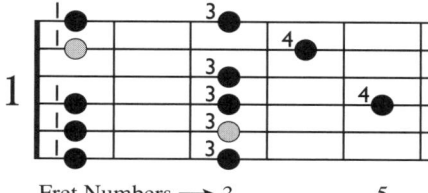

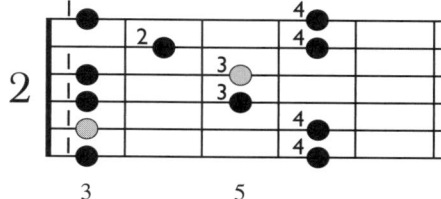

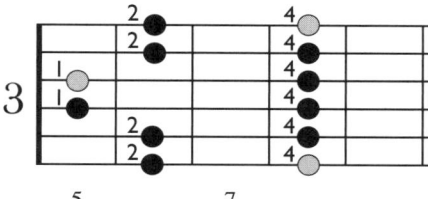

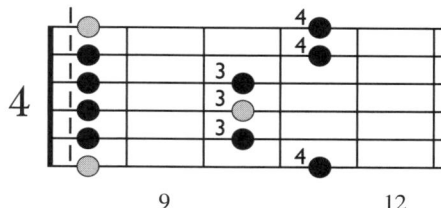

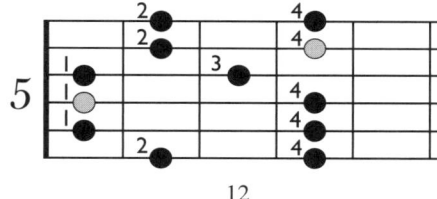

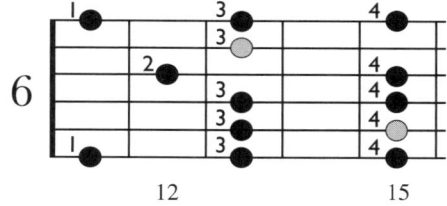

MAJOR PENTATONIC SCALES

Students are usually happy to hear that major pentatonic scales use the same fingerings as the minor pentatonic scales they have already learned. All they have to do is think of the root as being in a different place. If the student has had some fundamental theory training, you could explain that the relationship between the two scales is the same as that of relative major and minor keys. In other words, just as C Major and A Minor are related keys, the C Major Pentatonic scale is the same as an A Minor Pentatonic scale. An F Major Pentatonic scale contains the same notes as a D Minor Pentatonic scale and so on.

This is a good time to mention to your student that in quite a few instances the two scales (major and minor pentatonic) from the same root can be used interchangeably. In such cases the minor pentatonic scale will produce a more "bluesy" sound and the major pentatonic scale suggests a sweeter, "countryish" sound. On page 68 are some sample fingerings.

C Major Pentatonic Scale Forms

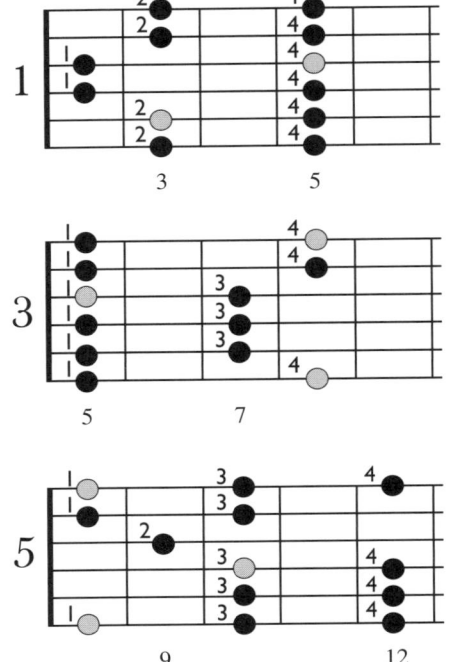

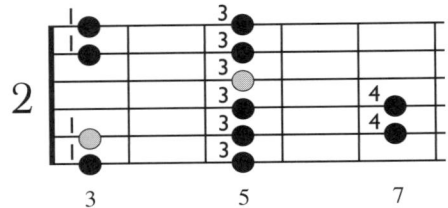

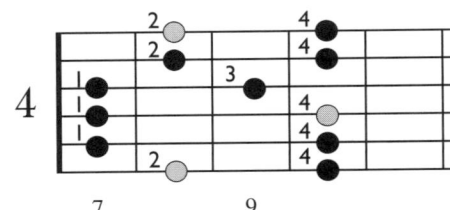

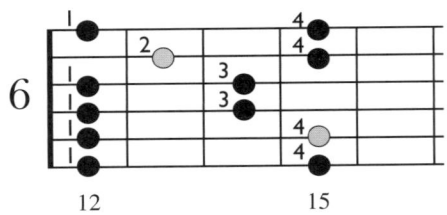

THE BLUES SCALE

The flat-5 that occurs in the blues scale gives the student a dramatic new sound with which to experiment. Explain that by adding this extra note to the minor pentatonic scale, they can suddenly sound much bluesier. Here are some blues scale fingerings.

C Blues Scale Forms

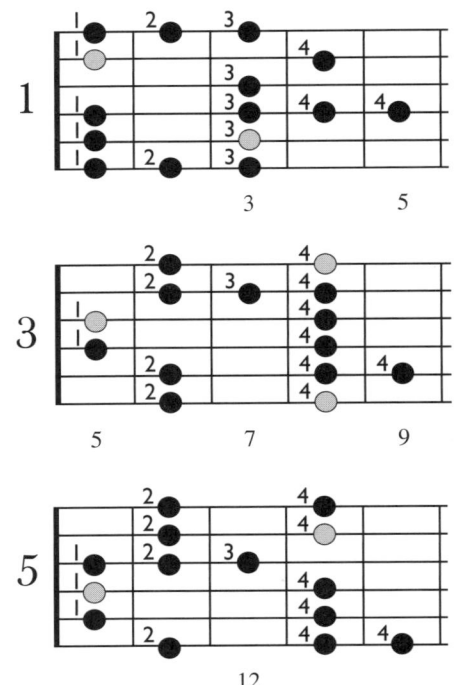

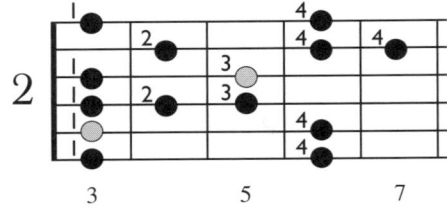

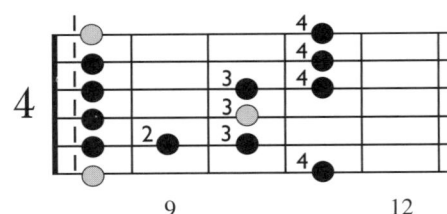

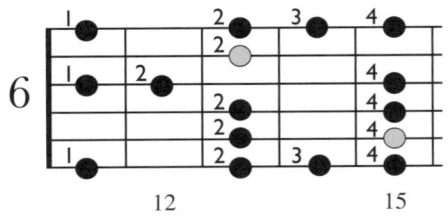

STARTING TO IMPROVISE

Improvising requires becoming adept at many different skills. Students should usually begin by improvising with scales because it's easy to come up with ideas that sound pretty good. Later on, we introduce concepts like starting phrases on chord tones, using licks and incorporating melodic patterns. Most students are a little nervous about improvising for the first time, but after a little experience they see how fun it can be.

It should be mentioned, there are a lot of ways to accelerate the student's progress with improvising. Most involve the use of software, recorders and play-along CDs. There is no doubt that students who practice with this technology will learn certain skills much faster than those who do not. Make sure your student knows that these options exist.

Backing Track—*Slow Blues*

Have your students improvise over this backing track. It is a slow 12-bar blues in A, with a $\frac{12}{8}$ feel. Here are the changes:

A / D9 / A / Emin11 A7#5 /
D9 / D#dim /A Bmin7 / C#min7 F#7♭9 /
E9 / D9 / A / E7#9 //

Backing Track—*Shuffle Blues*

This is a medium-tempo shuffle blues in G. The changes are:

G / C9 / G / G7 /
C9 / C9 / G7 / G7 /
D9 / C9 / G7 / G7 (D7)//

BECOMING FAMILIAR WITH THE SOUND OF THE SCALE

It is important for the student to become familiar with both the fingering and the sound of the scale. After making sure he/she is playing with good technique, have the student practice playing the scale from every root, up and down the fretboard. Keep the tempo and dynamics even.

The next step is to play a blues progression and let the student experiment by randomly playing notes from the scale. Do this for several minutes. It really doesn't matter what it sounds like at this point. The idea is for the student to start hearing the notes over the chord progression. You may want the student to practice doing this all week before moving on to any other improvising concepts. They'll think it's a fun assignment, and it is, but it's also a way to become well grounded in the sound and fingering of the scale.

EXPERIMENTING WITH TIME

One of the main reasons students often feel they are "stuck," playing the same ideas over and over when they improvise, is because they forget to utilize other skills and knowledge at their disposal. One of the most forgotten tools is the use of note duration. When your student first tried to improvise over the blues progression, he/she probably played quarter notes or didn't even pay much attention to time at all. However, once your students have the technical facility to play the scale correctly, you need to show them how to use various note values to create variety in their improvising. Many teachers use an exercise similar to the one that follows to help them with this.

1. Have your student improvise freely over a blues progression using any scale fingering they are comfortable with. Do this for several minutes to warm up.
2. Now have your students improvise with only whole notes. Do this until your student starts to run out of ideas.
3. Now tell your student to improvise with only half notes. When the ideas run dry, move on.
4. Now improvise with only whole and half notes combined.
5. Improvise with only quarter notes.
6. Improvise with quarter notes and half notes combined.
7. Improvise with quarter notes, half notes and whole notes combined.
8. If possible, have the student improvise with a steady stream of eighth notes.
9. Combine quarter notes and eighth notes.
10. Now let your student improvise freely again, using any combination of note values. Point out how much more interesting they sound now than when they improvised at the beginning of the exercise.

LEARNING AND USING LICKS

The topic of teaching licks is controversial among some teachers. Of course, we don't want our students to rely entirely on preconceived licks while improvising, but they can be quite beneficial for most students.

WHY TEACH LICKS?

When we first learn to speak, our parents teach us words that we later learn to put together into phrases. Learning licks is much like this. If you just play scales like most beginning improvisers do, it becomes apparent that a lot of the "good stuff" we hear is not really coming from this resource alone. Good improvisers use many different improvisational devices. Scales are one. Licks can be another.

The fear of course is that your student will simply connect one lick after another and think they are improvising, which they are not. In most cases, all it takes is to explain that improvising really consists of scales, arpeggios, licks, melodic patterns and flashes of inspiration, among other things. It's perfectly all right to study and practice licks—just don't let it become the central focus. Besides gaining valuable vocabulary, the student learns how different guitarists think in various improvisational situations. Learning licks tends to solidify a student's harmonic knowledge. Licks can be good chop-building exercises as well.

APPLYING LICKS

You can teach licks with a routine similar to this:

1. Have the student learn the lick slowly, using correct fingering and technique. Be sure the student knows what chord or chord progression the lick "works" over.

2. Once the student can play the lick, have him practice it in all keys like this: Play the appropriate chord, play the lick, play the chord again. Then move up one fret and repeat, moving eventually over the entire fretboard. Practicing like this reinforces both the lick and its context.

3. Practice using the lick over chord progressions in various keys. Soon the lick becomes part of your student's vocabulary.

Don't just have your students practice a lick chromatically up and down the fretboard, have them experiment, moving in whole steps, minor 3rds, 4ths and 5ths as well. Try to find signature licks from the best known blues players to teach your students. Teaching well-known licks can be a great motivator.

Following are some typical blues licks.

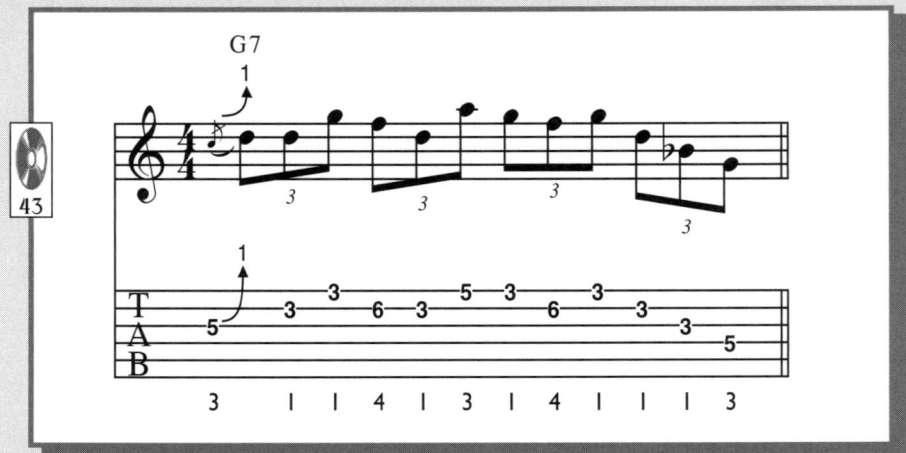

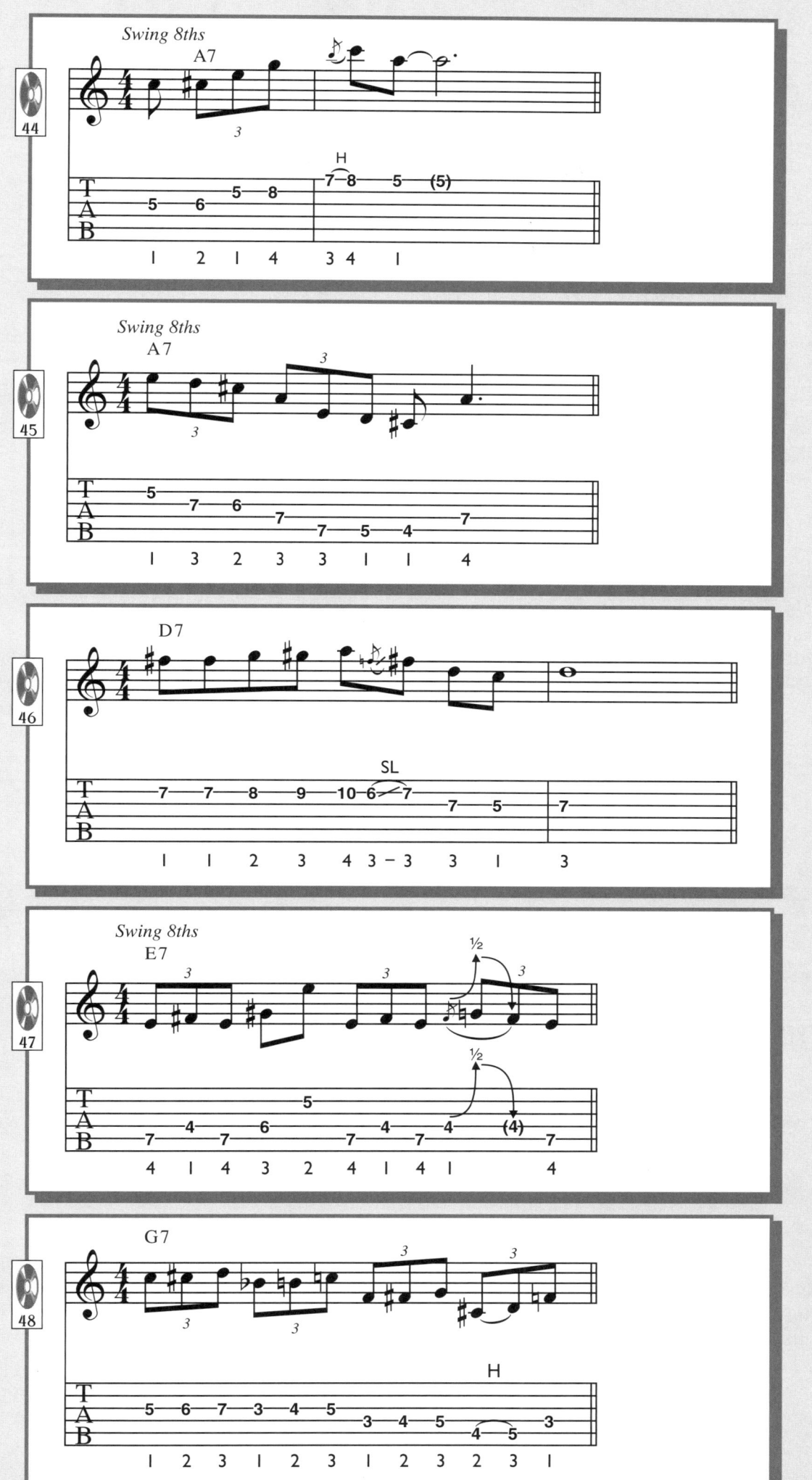

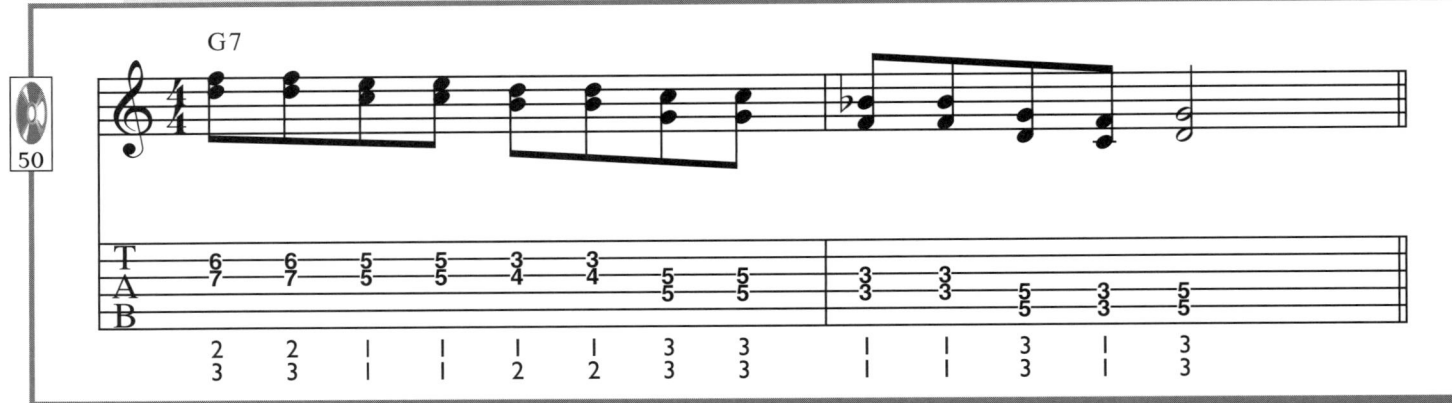

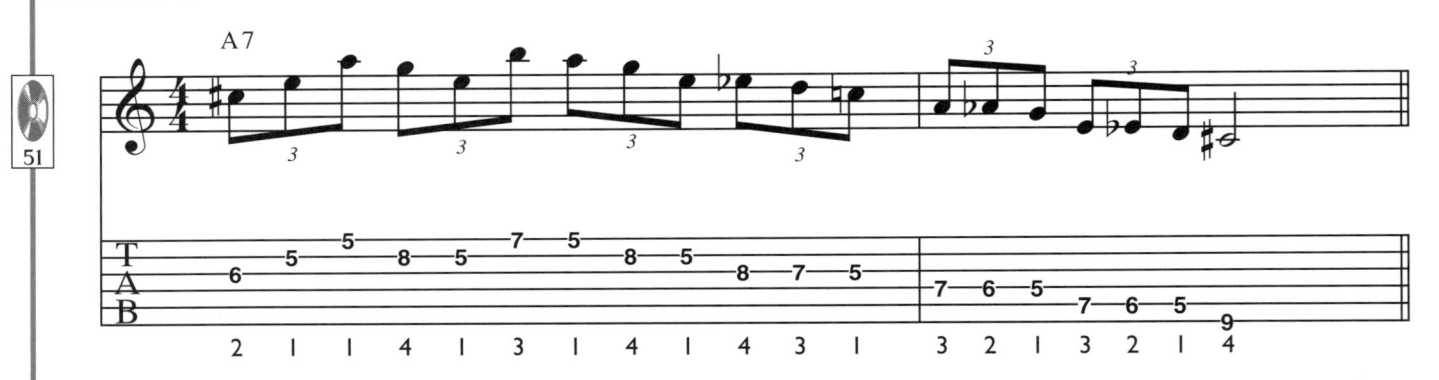

OTHER RELATED SKILLS FOR BLUES GUITAR STUDENTS

Blues students will invariably ask you questions about bending notes, playing fast, keeping time when playing a very slow blues, getting that "blues" sound, equipment and possibly where they can go to hear (or even play!) live blues. If you are teaching blues guitar, you should have clear, well thought-out answers for them.

LEARNING BLUES SONGS

Like with any other style, it is important to give your blues students lots of songs. Many students know their theory and can improvise, but many come up short when it comes to knowing songs. Everyone starts playing guitar because they want to play songs. Somehow, many students and teachers alike forget this. Your students will still learn the most from working on songs. They are the perfect vehicle for learning both theory and technique. Provide your students with a list of blues artists and CDs to which they should listen. Besides exposing them to the blues world, they will come to you with more and more questions. This, for most teachers, is part of the reward.

CHAPTER TEN
TEACHING ROCK GUITAR

As one would expect, rock students make up perhaps the largest segment of guitar students. One thing that complicates this for some teachers is that there are so many different types of rock music (classic rock, metal, hard rock, soft rock, oldies rock, punk, etc.). It's difficult for any teacher to be adept at all forms of rock guitar. Most of the varying forms of rock music have a lot in common, but their nuances distinguish them. If you don't keep up with these styles and their differences, you probably shouldn't try to teach these kinds of lessons. There is sometimes a whole "lifestyle" that goes with each of these rock forms. It's difficult to teach a style you may have trouble relating to.

The following sections deal primarily with the tools that are common to most forms of rock.

COMMON CHORDS USED IN ROCK GUITAR

Obviously, barre chords (see pages 57–59) make up the vast majority of chord forms used in rock music. Open position chords and other basic chords (see pages 50–51) are used extensively as well. Additional chords commonly found in rock are power chords, "add 9," "sus 2" and "sus 4" chords.

"...rock students make up perhaps the largest segment of guitar students."

POWER CHORDS

Power chords first became popular in the 1970s and have been widely used ever since. They are two-note chords comprised of a root and the note a perfect 5th higher. The are commonly labeled with the root-name and the number "5," as in "G5," or "C5." They produce a rather gothic and harmonically ambiguous sound that has become synonymous with modern rock music. One of the main benefits of using power chords is that many more types of scales and licks can be played over them. Since there are no defining (or confining) 3rds or 7ths in the chord, one can approach improvisation with a much freer attitude. Compared with other kinds of pop music or jazz, rock improvisation has more to do with an overall effect than melodic development in many cases. The two common forms of power chords are shown below:

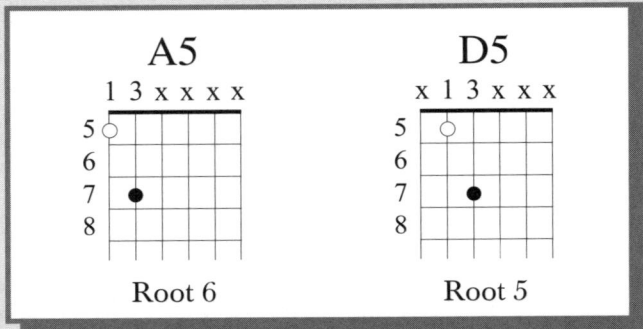

Some players prefer to double the root, as shown in these examples:

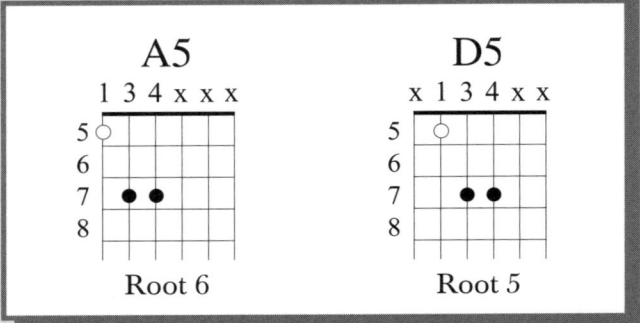

ADD 9 AND SUSPENDED 2 CHORDS

While related, add 9 and sus 2 chords are not quite the same thing.

Add 9 chords are found in all kinds of music. They consist of a major or minor triad with a 9th added. These chords sound light, but still have a lush quality to them. Where in the chord you decide to place the 9th makes all the difference.

Placed on top, they produce a brighter sound like with the examples below and at the top of the next page:

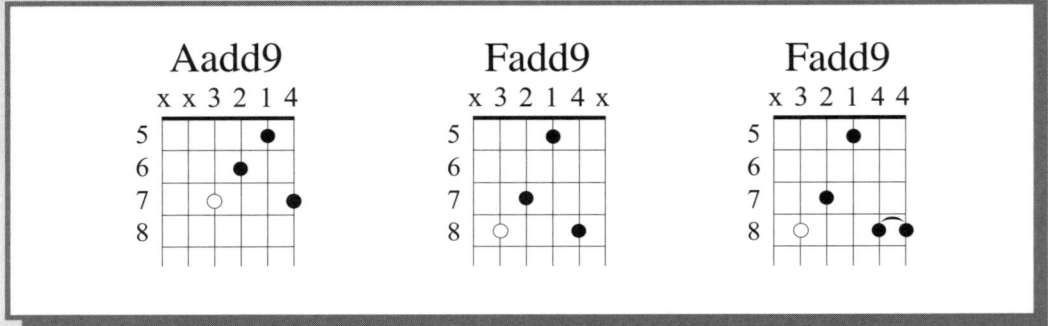

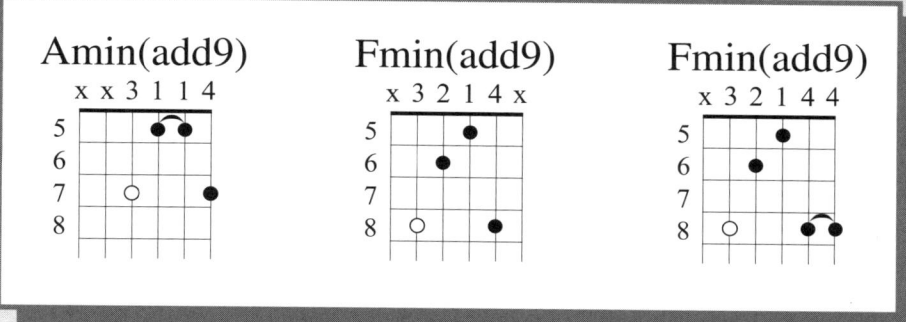

Placed in the middle, the chords have a more complex sound because of the minor 2nd produced in minor chords, and the major 2nd produced in major chords. The group Steely Dan has commonly substituted these instead of straight major and minor chords for years. In fact, it's an important part of their overall sound.

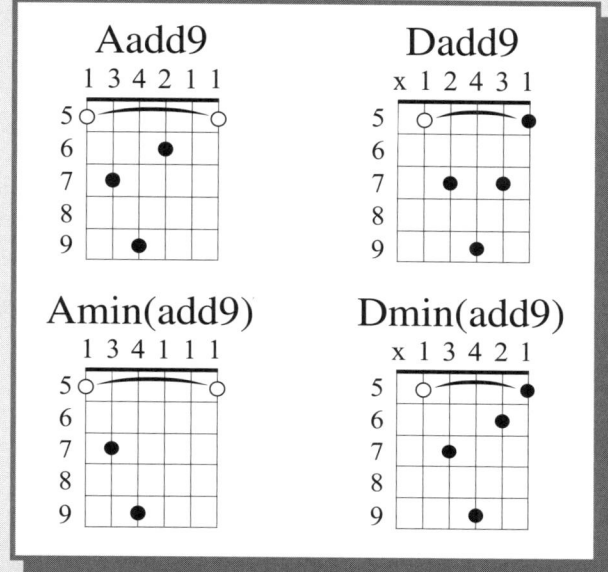

"Suspended 2" chords are a little different. In most cases, the "2" or "9" replaces the 3rd of the chord producing a completely open sounding texture. Here are some examples:

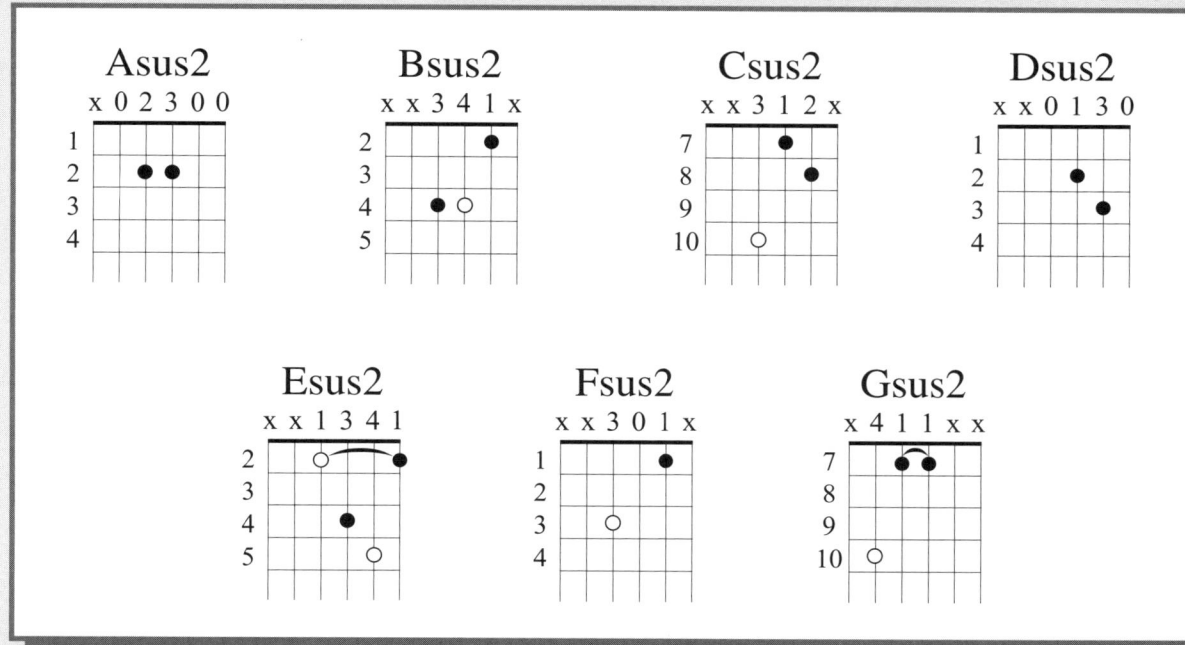

SUSPENDED 4 CHORDS

Suspended 4, or "sus 4" chords are found in all styles of music. To form one, simply replace the 3rd of the chord with the 4th. This chord's function is to provide some tension within the chord progression. Sus 4 chords almost always resolve to a dominant 7th or major chord with the same root, by lowering the 4th back down to the 3rd. In other words, G7sus4 will usually resolve to G7. Dsus4 will usually resolve to D Major. Most students will remember these chords better if you teach them along with the resolution. Shown below are a few suspended 4 chords with some common resolutions.

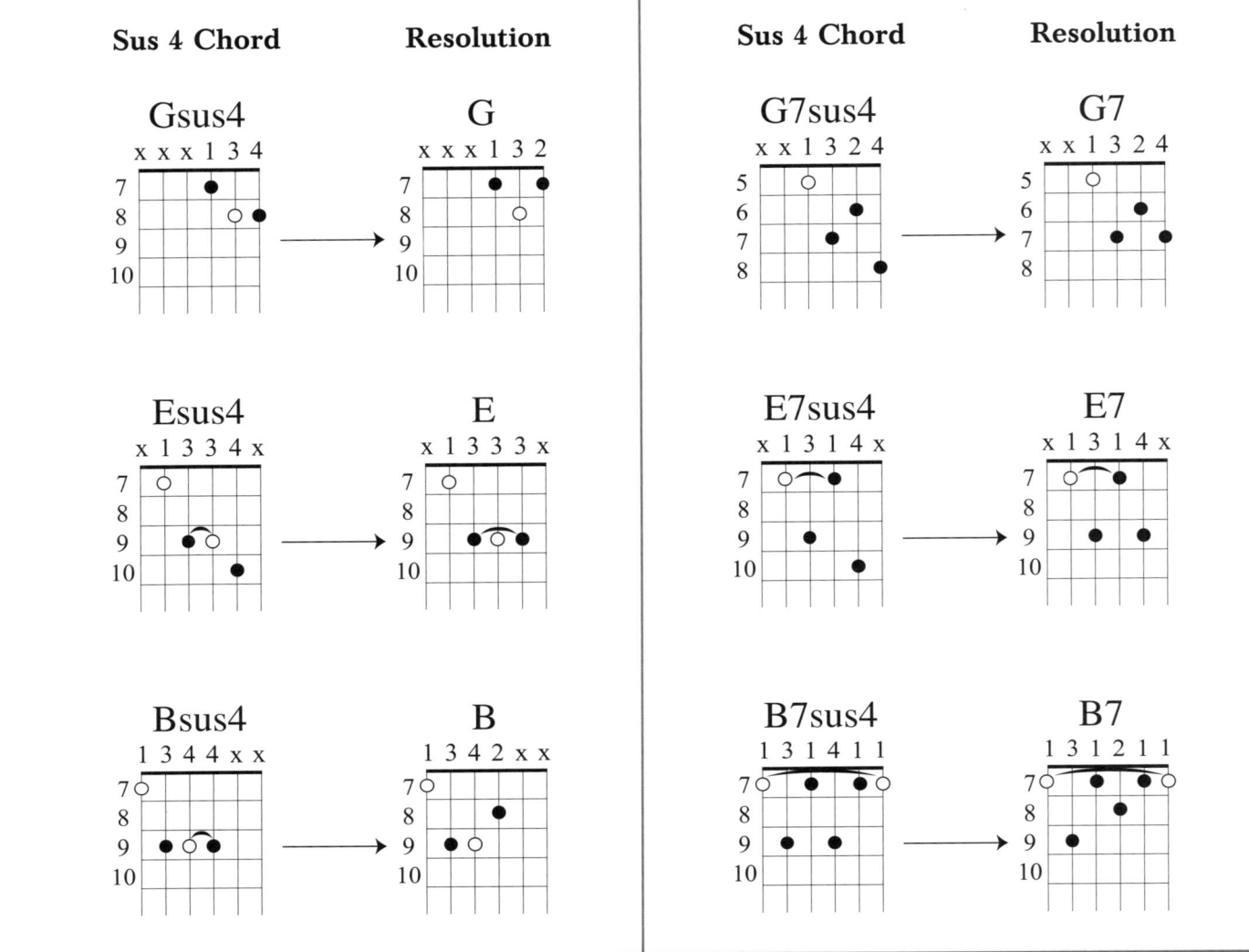

ROCK PROGRESSIONS

Most types of popular music depend on a certain amount of repetition when it comes to chord progressions—and rock is no exception. Thousands of rock tunes are based on the chord progressions that follow. What distinguishes one song from another is often a matter of instrumentation, energy, tonal color, melody, arrangement and lyric. If your students become familiar with the following chord progressions, they'll have a pretty good overview of the genre.

I–IV–V PROGRESSIONS

The basics of this chord progression were covered in Chapter Nine (Teaching Blues Guitar, pages 61–63). In many rock tunes based on this chord progression, a melodic riff is being played rather than actual chords. The riff outlines the harmony so we feel like we're hearing the actual chord. In reality, the chords are only being implied. It is also very common for one guitarist in a band to play chords while a second guitarist is playing the riff. Learning actual songs is the best way to learn about these techniques, but you may want to introduce the idea with short I–IV–V riffs like the ones that follow:

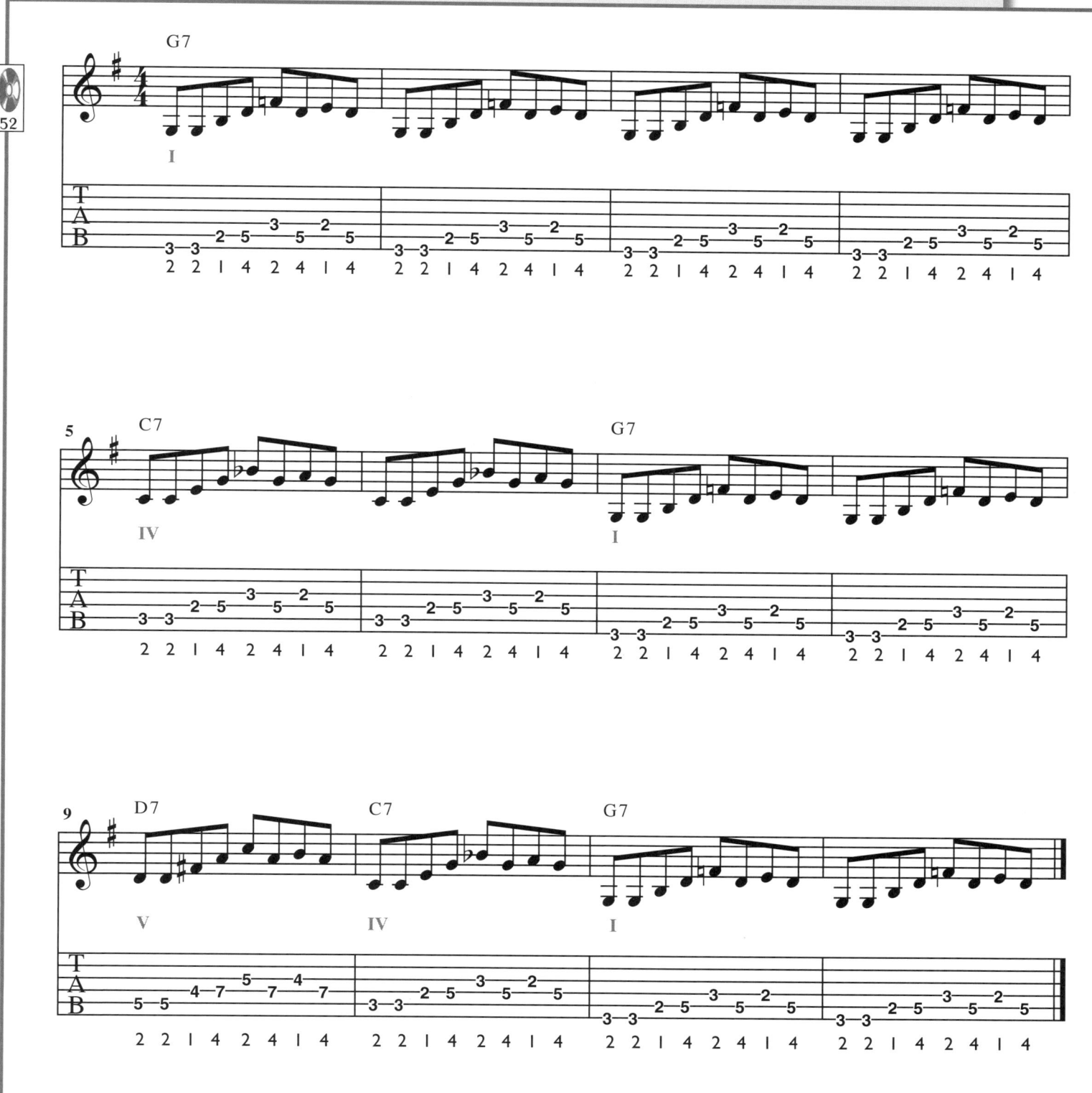

Teaching Guitar • **77**

I–vi–IV–V PROGRESSIONS

The I–vi–IV–V progression is yet another progression that has spawned thousands of rock and roll songs—especially rock ballads of the 1950s. Like the I–IV–V progression, it is the *way* it is played that makes one song different from another. In most rock situations, the arrangement and chord voicings themselves can be integral parts of the song. Following are some typical examples of the I–vi–IV–V progression in a rock context:

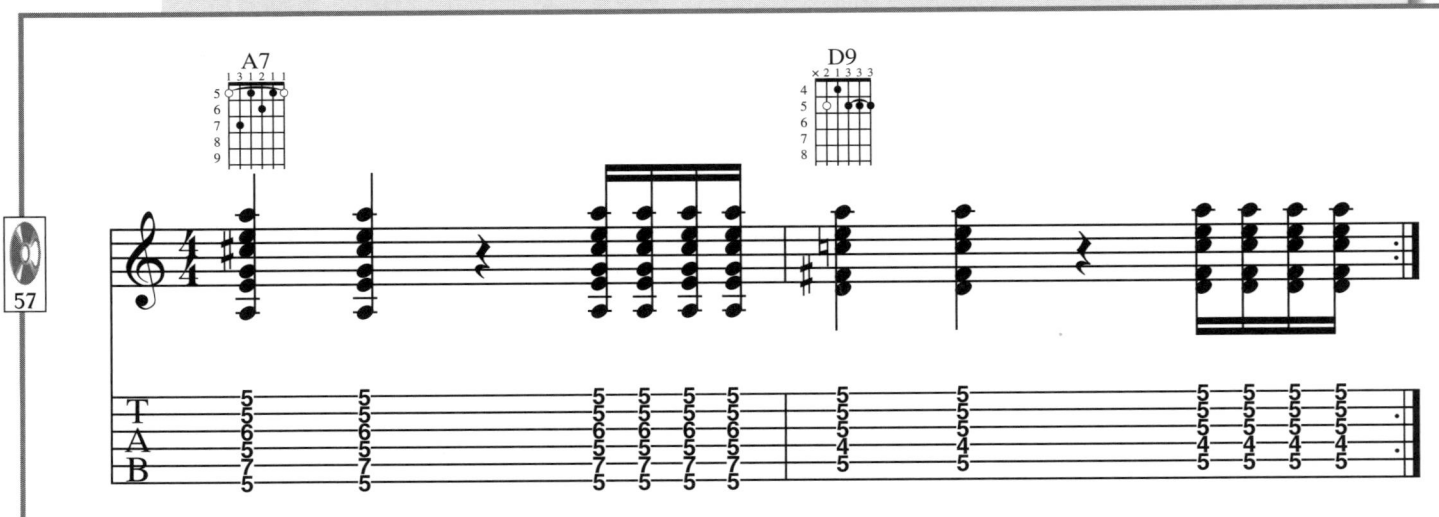

ONE- AND TWO-CHORD VAMPS

Vamps consisting of only one or two chords have been around a long time. In most cases, they are temporary interludes between two sections of music. In rock, entire songs are sometimes based on them. Here are some examples that should sound familiar.

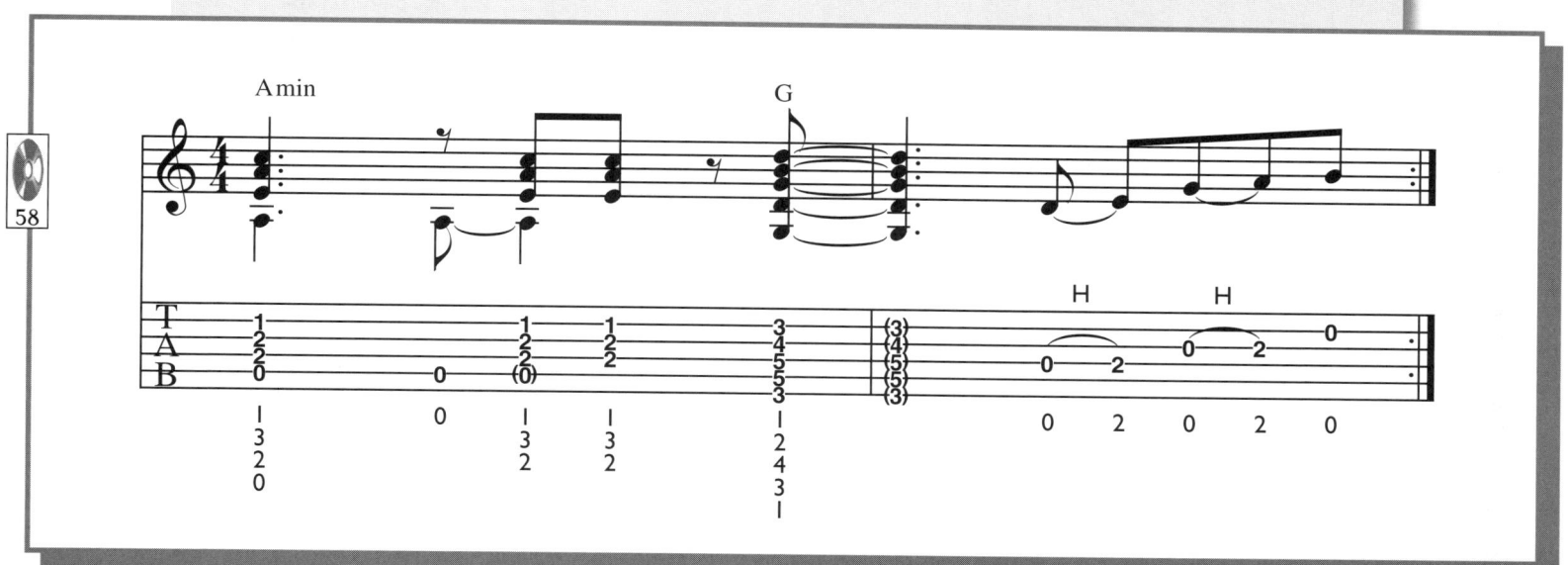

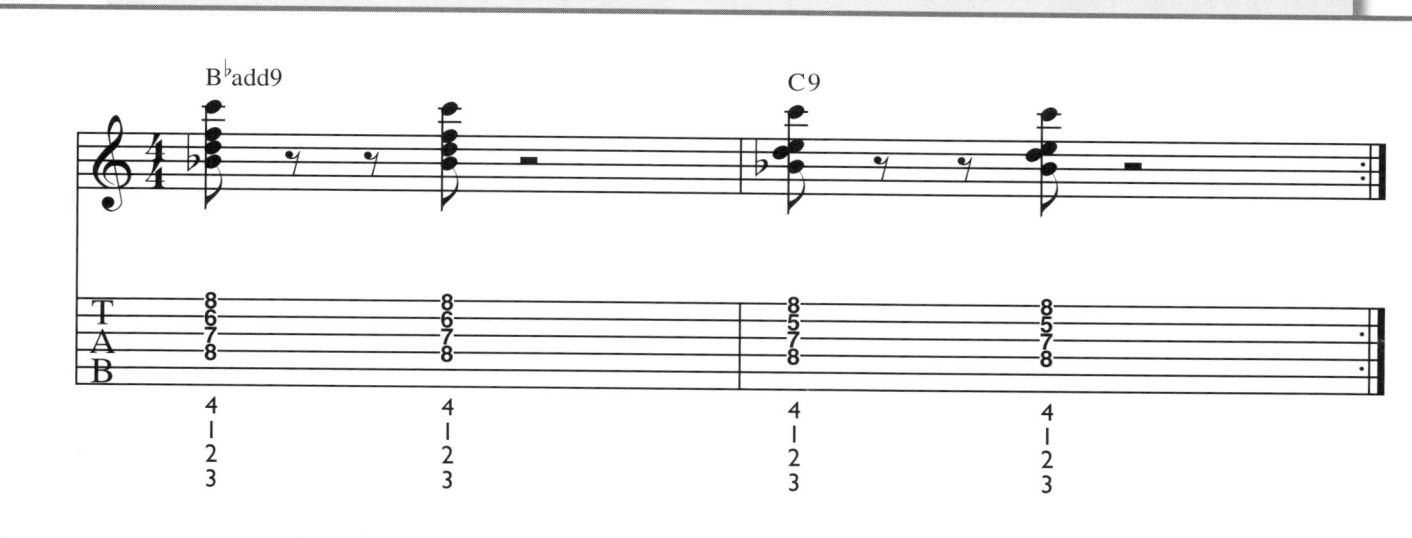

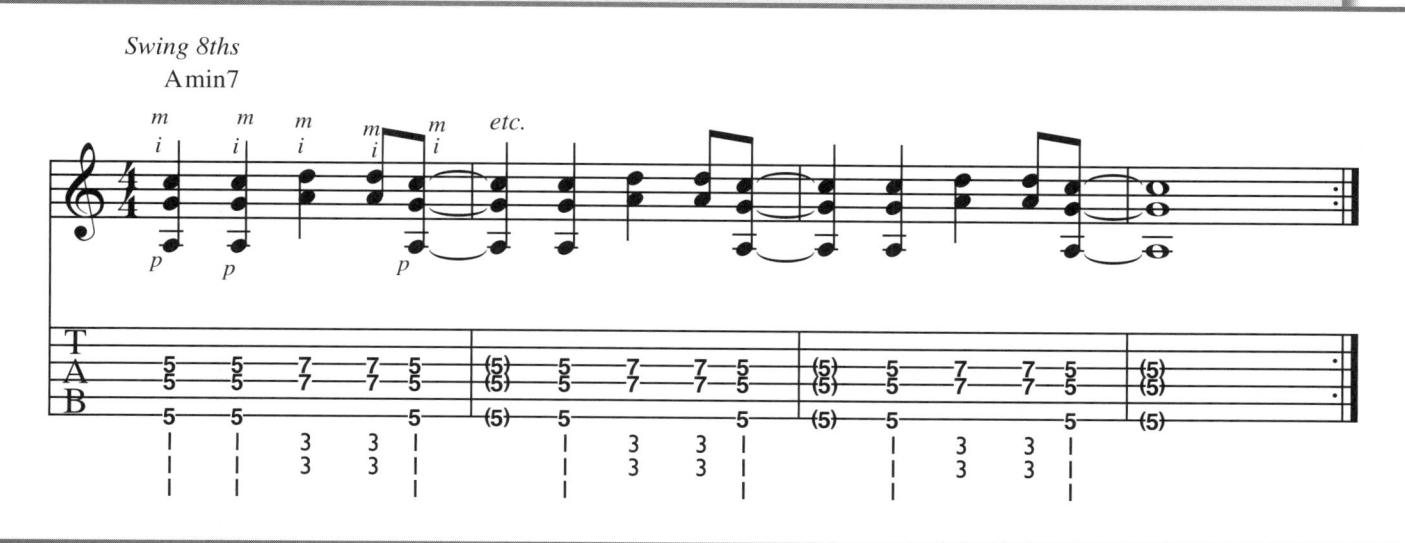

CHORD-RIFF PROGRESSIONS

There are many rock tunes that do not rely on typical diatonic chord progressions. Instead, they can be based on repetitive movements of barre or power chords along the guitar fretboard; these are chord-riffs. This has resulted in quite a few unorthodox chord progressions that have become very popular. Sometimes songs can be built entirely on these chord-riff ideas by using different chord-riffs for different parts of the song. Following are some examples that should sound familiar:

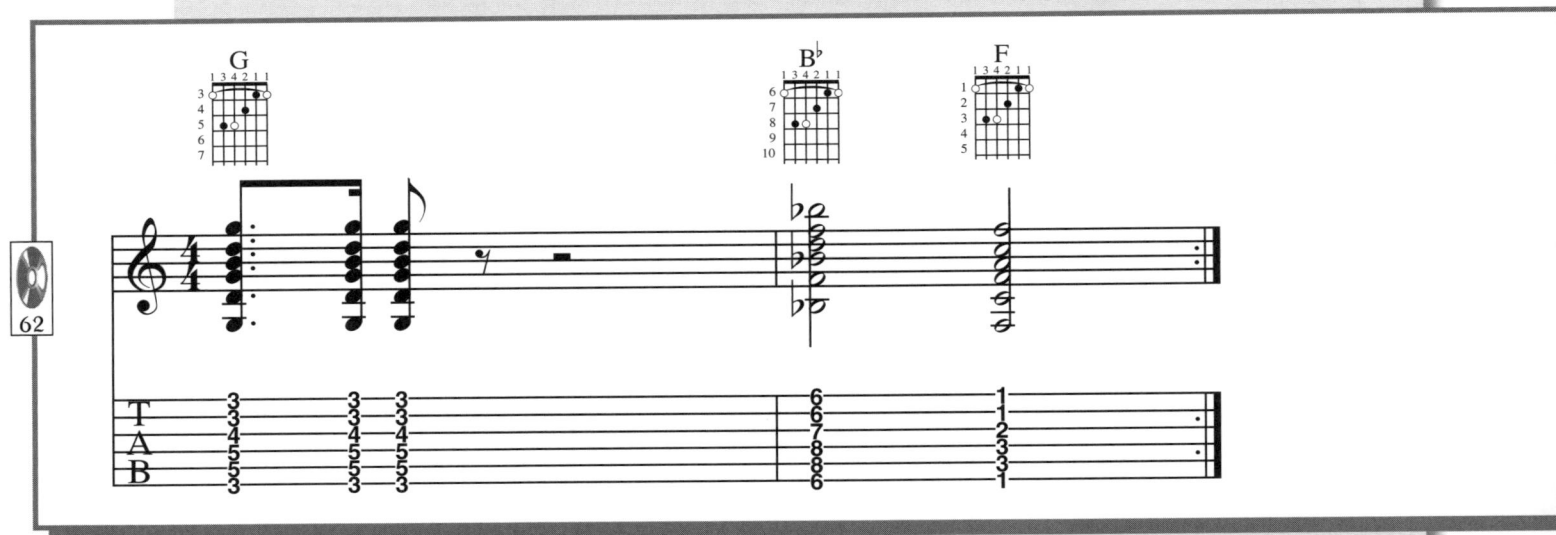

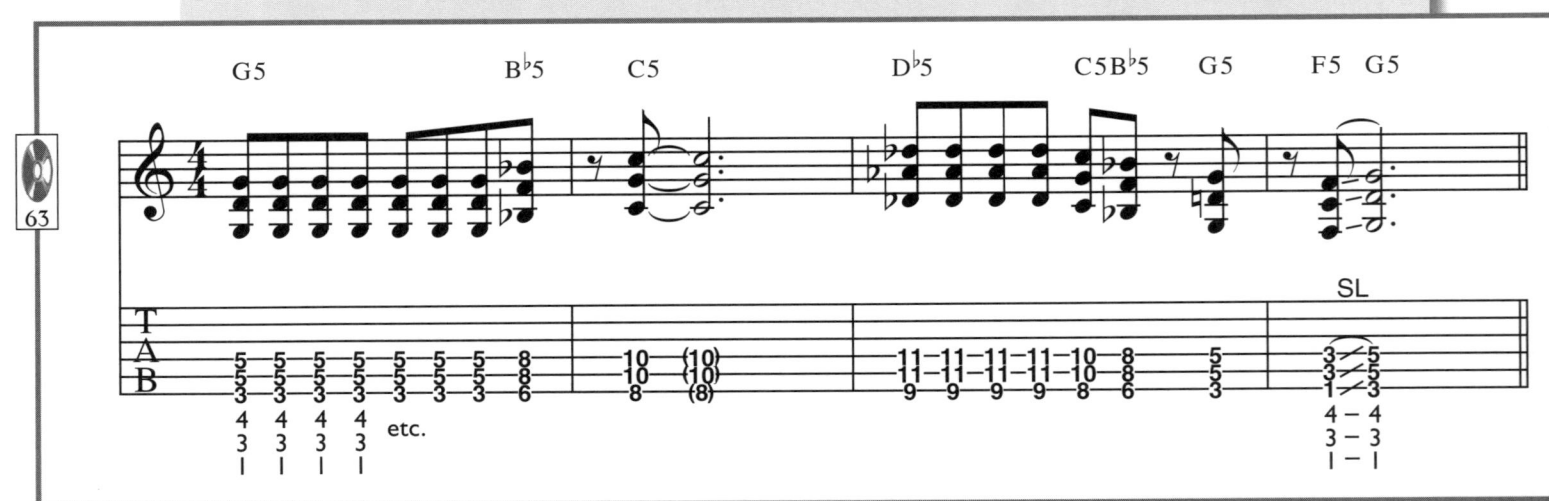

ROCK RHYTHM PATTERNS

The songs your students want to learn should provide you with many different rhythms to work on. You may also want to introduce them to basic rock patterns like these:

SCALES FOR ROCK

Most rock improvising is based on scales and modes. The more fingerings your students know for each important rock scale, the more flexibility and control they will have over their leads.

THE BLUES AND PENTATONIC SCALES

The blues and pentatonic scales have already been discussed in Chapter Nine (Teaching Blues Guitar, pages 66–68). The same rules of engagement apply when using these scales in a rock format.

THE MAJOR SCALE

The major scale is an important scale in rock because it adds a much different melodic flavor than the blues and pentatonic scales. It's great for contrast in a solo. Rock students need to know about this scale because it introduces them to diatonic harmony and modes. When teaching rock students about the major scale, be sure to cover:

- Five or six scale fingerings.
- Harmonizing the scale in triads (with fingerings).
- Harmonizing the scale in 7th chords (with fingerings).
- Transposing chord progressions.

There are many systems for applying the major scale on the guitar. Choose one and make sure your students practice with consistent fingerings. Below and at the top of the next page are six fingerings you can use to get them started.

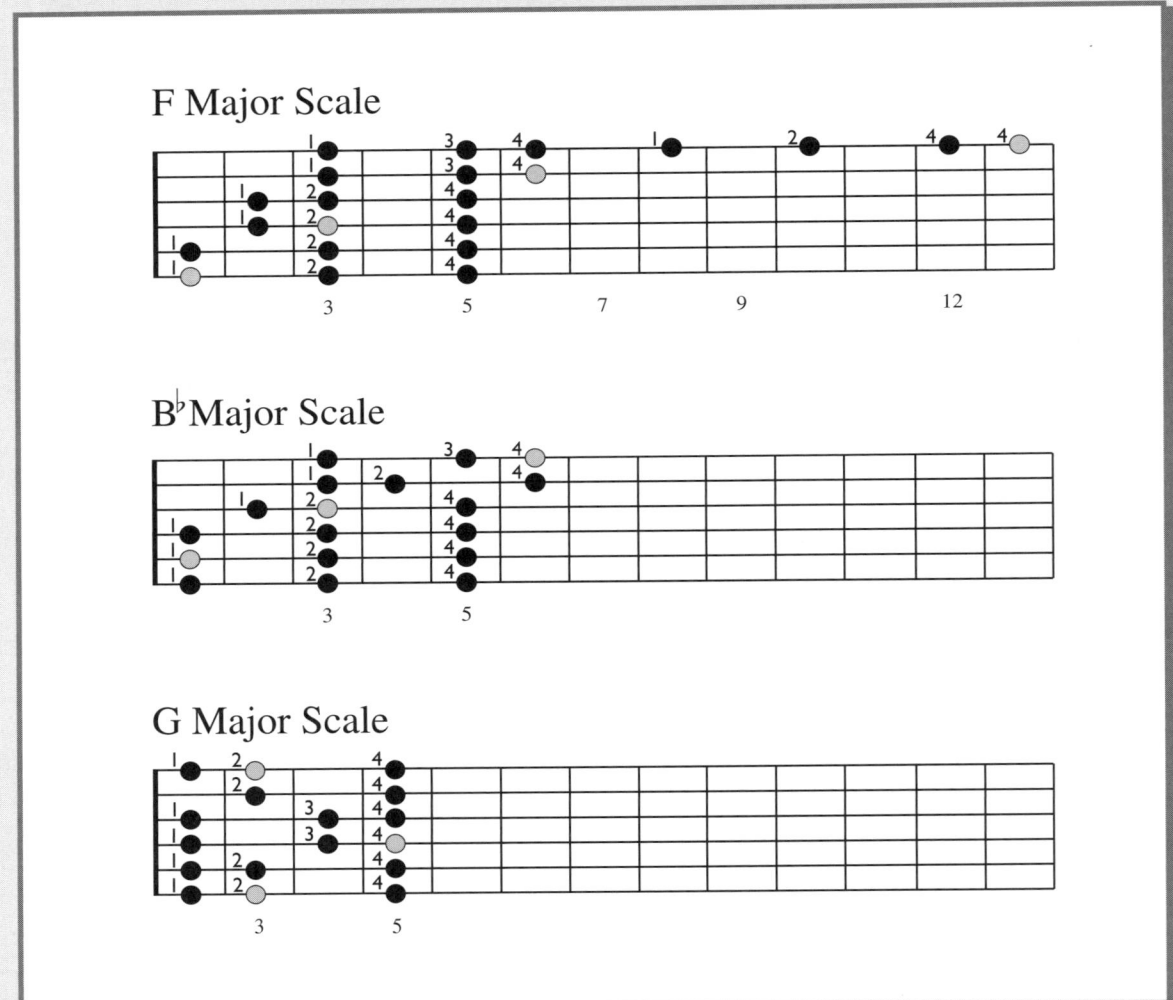

F Major Scale

B♭ Major Scale

G Major Scale

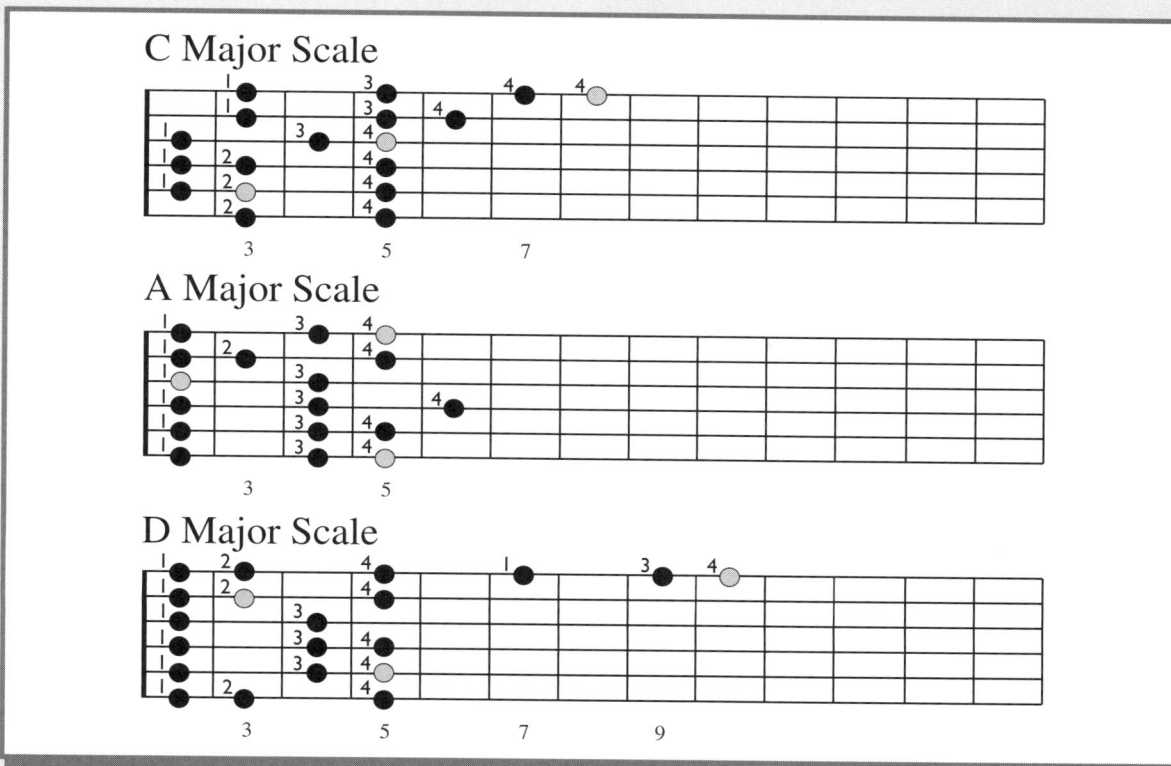

C Major Scale

A Major Scale

D Major Scale

MODES OF THE MAJOR SCALE

The next area of study for most rock students would be the modes of the major scale. Explain that the first mode, Ionian, is the major scale itself. Then explain that each mode corresponds to the diatonic chord that shares the root of the mode. In other words, play the D Dorian mode over the corresponding D Minor chord, the F Lydian mode over the F Major chord, etc. Remind them that the modes are additional scales they can use along with their other improvisational tools. Take your time here. Many students find the modes confusing. Under-teach by covering a single fingering of a particular mode during a lesson. This will make it easier for them to assimilate this information. Below and at the top of the next page are two fingerings for each mode.

MODES OF THE MAJOR SCALE

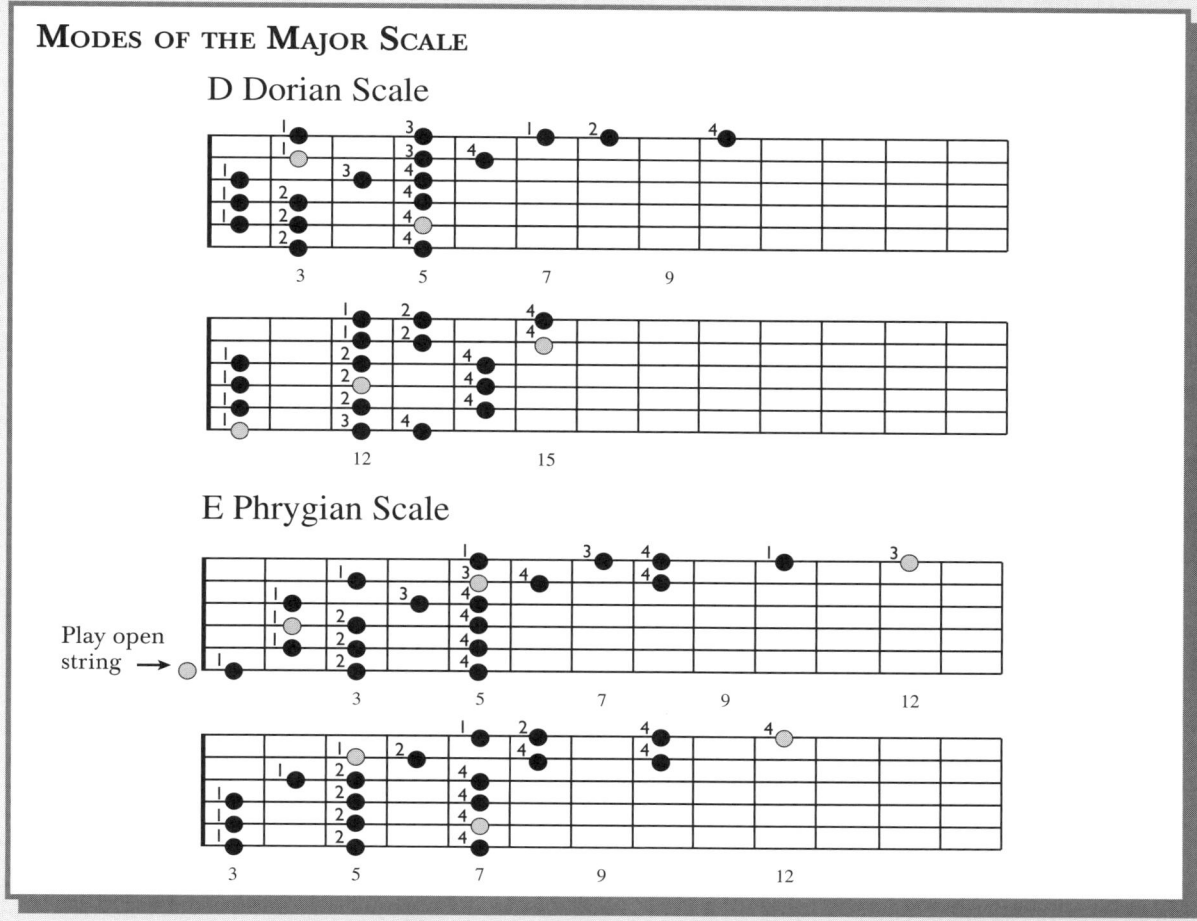

D Dorian Scale

E Phrygian Scale

Play open string →

F Lydian Scale

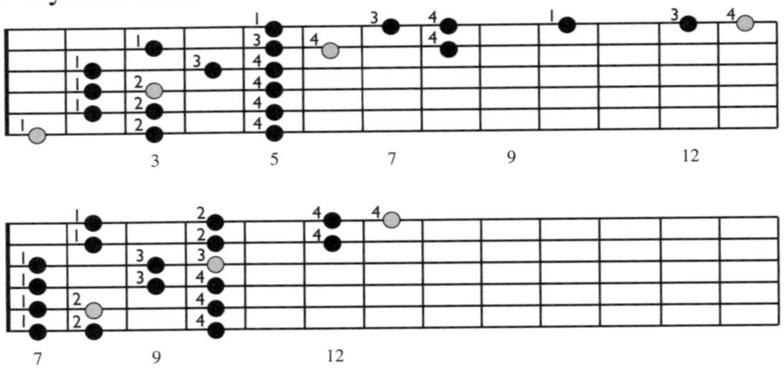

G Mixolydian Scale

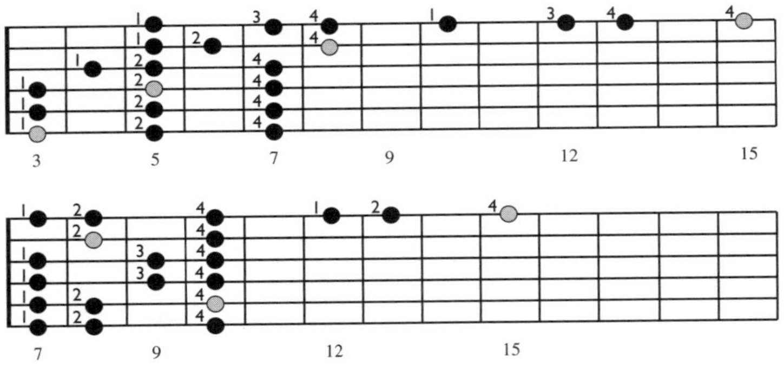

A Aeolian Scale

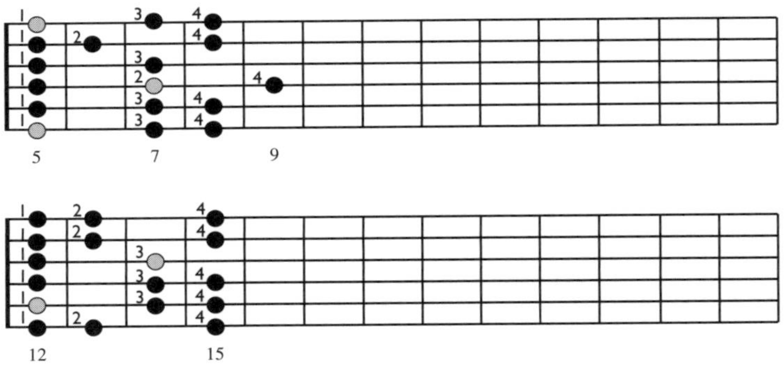

B Locrian Scale

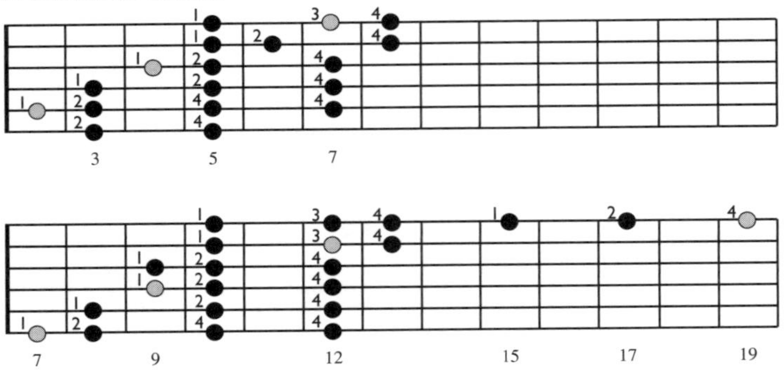

THE PHRYGIAN DOMINANT SCALE

This is an important scale to know if you teach "shredder" type rock students. The Phrygian dominant scale is actually the fifth mode of the harmonic minor scale. While it works in several different applications, your students will probably relate to it most when played over "5" type chords (power chords) that share the same root. In other words, use an A Phrygian Dominant scale over an A5 chord. Here are a couple fingerings to get things rolling.

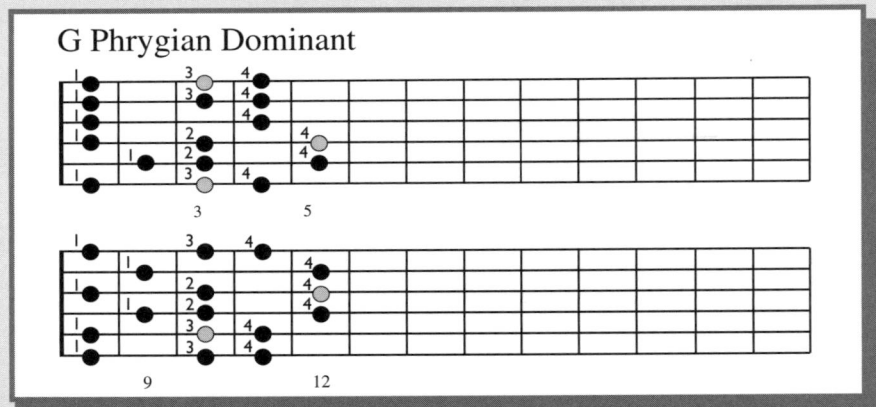

G Phrygian Dominant

Backing Track—*Slow Rock*

This is a medium two-chord vamp for your students to improvise over:

70

Gmin / C //

Backing Track—*Hard Rock*

Here's a familiar four-chord vamp:

71

Amin / G / F / F G//

ROCK LICKS

Rock students need licks for vocabulary and chop building just like blues students do. Here are some basic licks for new rock students.

OTHER RELATED TOPICS FOR ROCK STUDENTS

Your students will also want to know about: effects, cords, amps, etc.; whammy bar technique; home recording; string bending and vibrato; chicken pickin'; developing speed.

As we all know, rock sounds best when played fairly loud. Tell your students about the importance of earplugs. Who will tell them if you don't?

LEARNING ROCK TUNES

Unless your new students have a clear idea of the style of rock they want to learn, you'll probably want to start them off with classic rock tunes. These songs work well because they are familiar to almost everyone and require many of the same skills that are found in other forms of rock music. Your success in teaching other kinds of rock will depend on how familiar you are with the style.

CHAPTER ELEVEN
TEACHING JAZZ GUITAR

Teaching jazz is a little different than teaching most other styles. For one thing, students who come to jazz have usually been playing guitar a while already. For many people, jazz is an acquired taste. When blues and rock students start looking for a little more challenge in their guitar studies, they often gravitate to jazz. Jazz students usually realize they'll be working on certain materials over a lifetime, so their perspective is a lot different than the student who wants to learn the new No. 1 pop song every week. This is not to put other styles down in any way. It's just that it takes a different level of commitment to learn jazz because progress, for the most part, is relatively slow compared to other styles.

There is much to teach jazz students. Most teachers' methods are based to a large extent on how they were taught. This chapter outlines only the broadest areas that should be addressed.

TEACHING CHORDAL CONCEPTS

It is unusual for complete beginners to take jazz guitar lessons. If your student is not familiar with basic open position chords, barre chords, strumming or improvising in a blues or rock context, you may want to suggest that they take some time to develop some of these skills first.

The chordal concepts that follow represent only the tip of the harmonic iceberg in jazz, but are topics that students must master before moving on to more advanced jazz studies.

"When blues and rock students start looking for a little more challenge in their guitar studies, they often gravitate to jazz. Jazz students usually realize they'll be working on certain materials over a lifetime..."

HARMONIZED MAJOR SCALES

It is important for the student to know the chords that are natural to each major key. First, discuss the general theory behind this idea on paper. Later, show them how to generate fingerings for these harmonized scales along the fretboard.

The following sample fingerings can help get the ball rolling for your beginning jazz student.

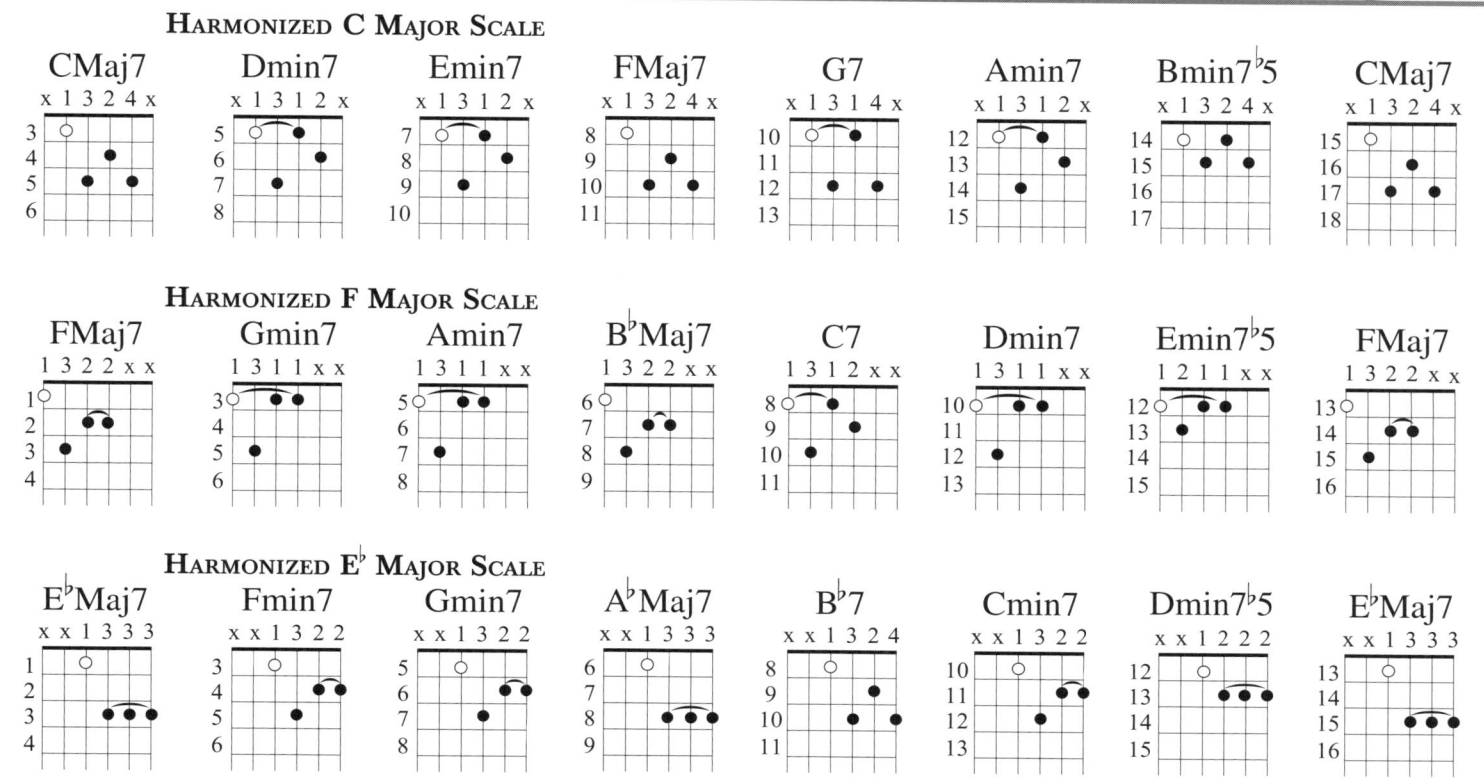

You can have your students build harmonized major scales starting with each of the following major chord forms.

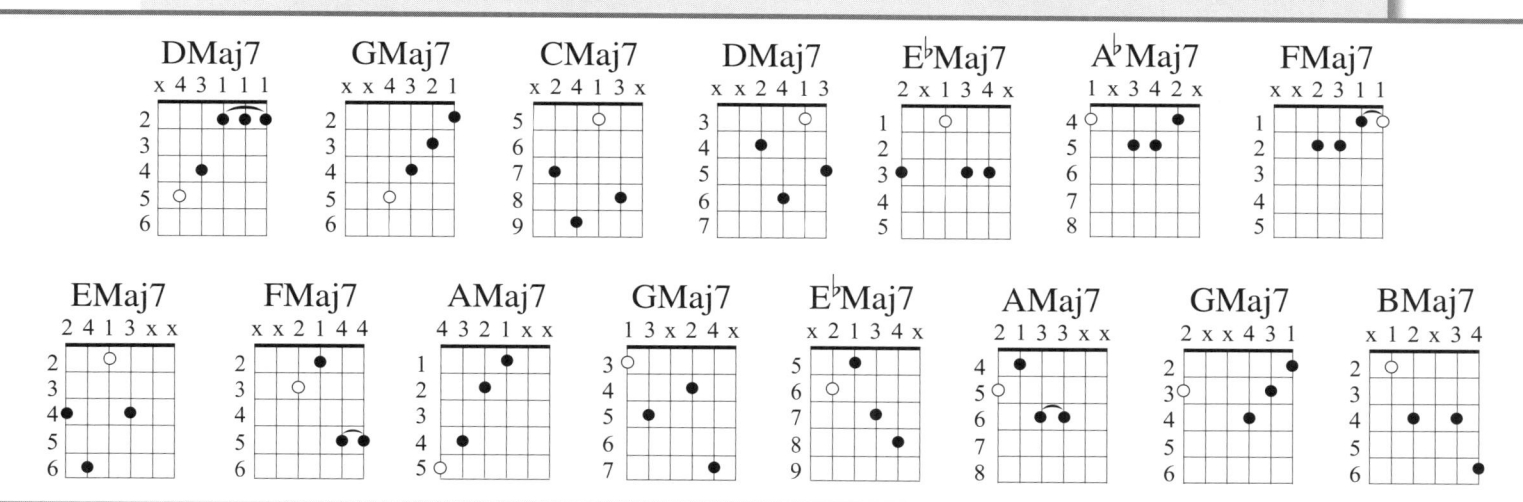

HARMONIZED MINOR SCALES

Most students successfully complete harmonized major scale studies. Applying the same ideas to minor scales is where many teachers and students drop the ball. If your students seem burnt out from working on all the major scale harmonies, move on to another topic for a while before assigning the same kind of work with the minor scales.

At the top of the next page are two examples of the harmonized harmonic minor scale, which is the same as the natural minor scale (Aeolian mode) with a ♮7.

HARMONIZED F HARMONIC MINOR SCALE

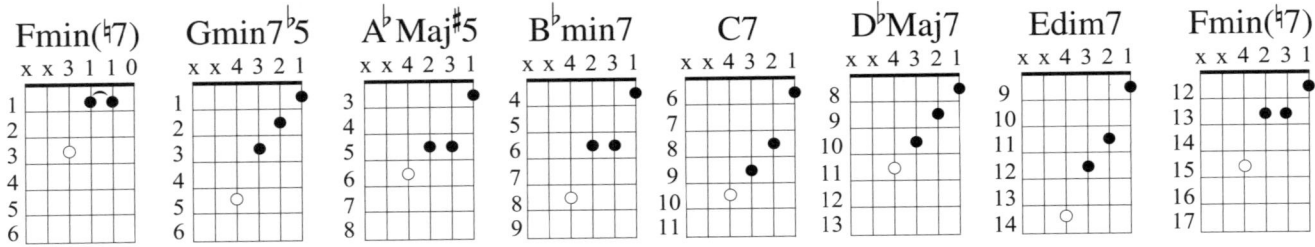

HARMONIZED B♭ HARMONIC MINOR SCALE

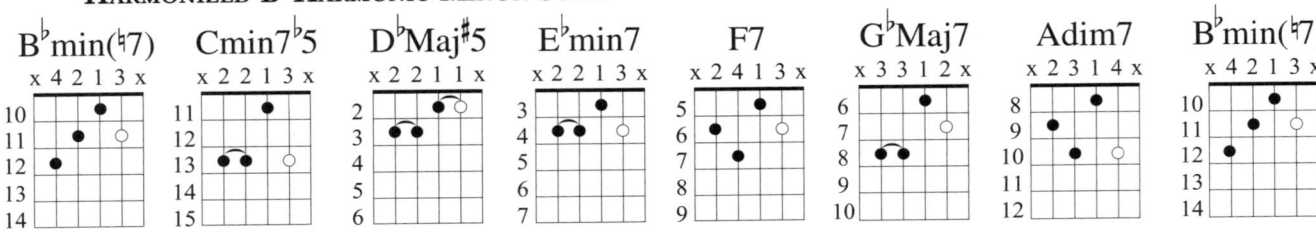

Have your students build harmonized harmonic minor scales from the following minor chords:

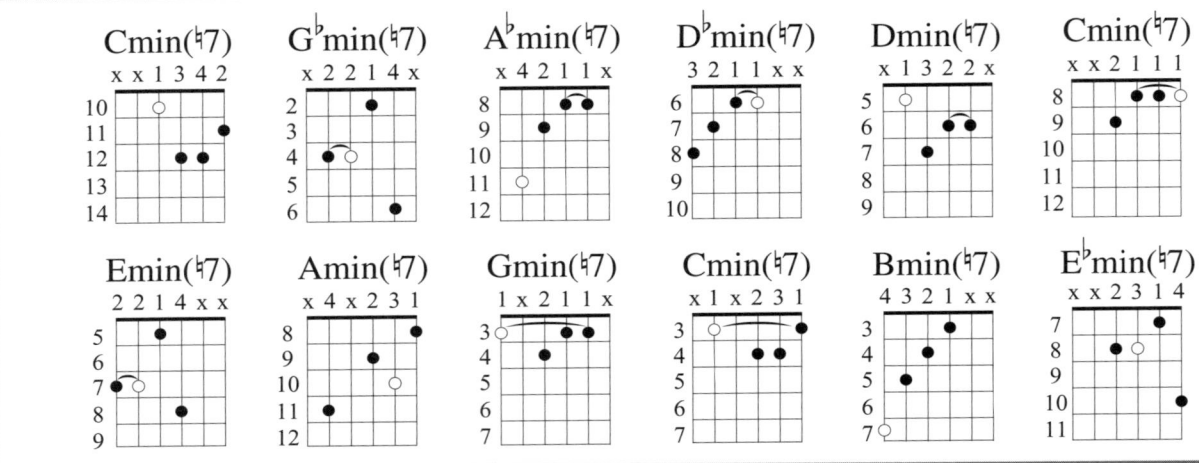

HARMONIZED MELODIC MINOR SCALE

The melodic minor scale is the same as the natural minor scale (Aeolian mode) with a ♮6 and ♮7. Here are two examples of the harmonized melodic minor scale.

HARMONIZED C MELODIC MINOR SCALE

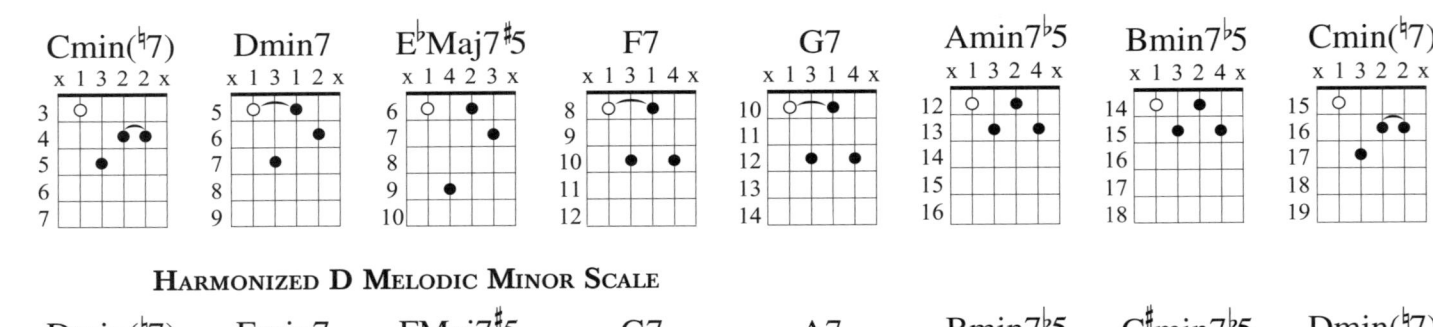

HARMONIZED D MELODIC MINOR SCALE

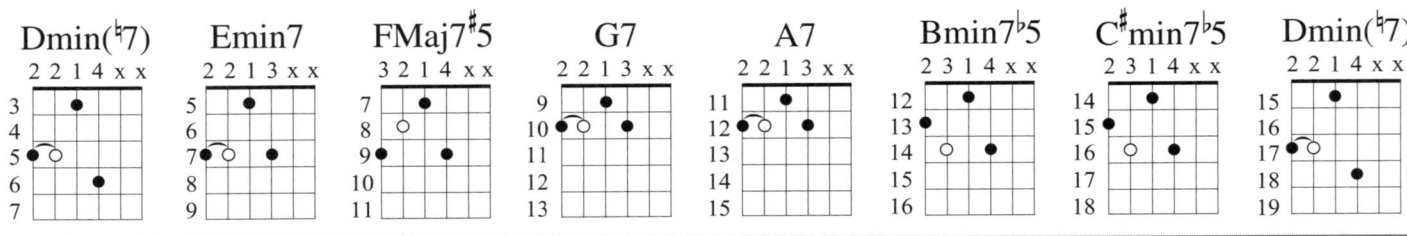

Have your students build harmonized melodic minor scales from all the minor natural-7 (♮7) chords in the middle of this page.

TRAVELING ii–V–I PROGRESSIONS

One of the main differences between jazz and many other kinds of music is its use of the ii–V–I progression. Between 1930 and 1970, thousands of jazz tunes and popular standards were based on this progression. One of the techniques used by songwriters of that era was to build songs on a series of ii–V–I progressions. Once you demonstrate this to your students, the harmonic complexity of jazz tunes and standards becomes much easier for them to understand. In fact, most students are a little relieved to find there is a system for all the seemingly unrelated chords in these tunes. Show them standards like "Misty" or "The Christmas Song." Eventually your student must memorize the ii–V–I progression in every key so they recognize it when analyzing chord progressions of songs. If they can't do this, they won't get very far in their jazz studies.

A good approach to teaching these concepts could go something like this:

1. Teach your student the basics of diatonic harmony: major scale construction, triads, 7th chords and harmonizing the major scale.

2. Explain to the student that most styles of music favor certain chord progressions. In blues and rock, it's the I–IV–V progression. In straight ahead jazz, it's the ii–V–I progression.

3. The student should now memorize the ii–V–I progression in every key. Most jazz concepts are studied in circle of 4ths order.

4. Show the student, in songs they know, how ii–V–I progressions travel through several keys.

5. Start assigning fingerings for ii–V–I progressions in all octaves, positions and string sets.

Here are some examples with which to start your students.

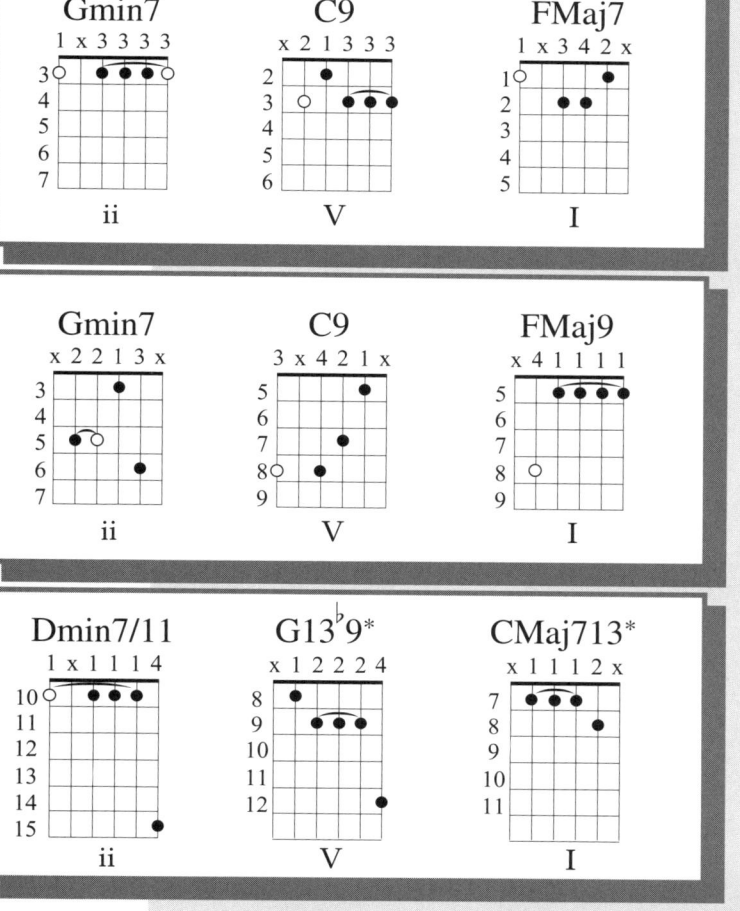

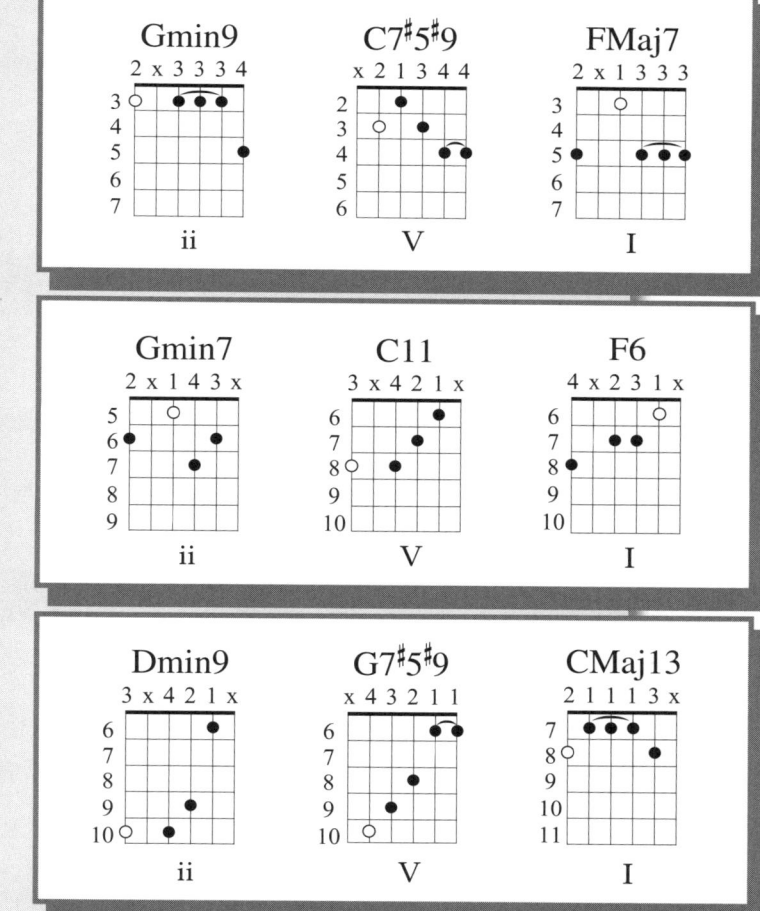

* This fingering does not include the root of the chord.

ALTERED DOMINANT CHORDS

To the beginning jazz student, there seems to be an endless list of altered dominant chords. Even chord names like B♭7♯5♭9 can be intimidating at first, so you want to make sure your student grows into this knowledge at a reasonable rate.

Before embarking on this journey, make sure your students are comfortable building triads, 7th chords and extended chords. They should know plenty of voicings, the theory behind them and how to use them on the guitar.

Tell them the only notes that can be altered are the 5th and 9th. Show them that if they alter any other tone in the chord, it becomes redundant to something already in the chord or scale. When they know they will only see alterations to the 5th and 9th, they won't feel quite so intimidated.

The alterations can be listed like this to show there really are *limited* possibilities:

- C7♭5 (could also be C9♭5)
- C7♯5 (could also be C9♯5)
- C7♭9
- C7♯9
- C7♭5♭9
- C7♯5♯9
- C7♭5♯9
- C7♯5♭9

Next you need to explain that they will often see chords with a ♯11 in them. Explain that, to a guitarist, a ♯11 is often treated as a ♭5 because of fingering limitations on the instrument.

Give them a lot of songs to work on. They should practice substituting dominant 7th chords with altered dominant chords. They will probably wonder why some of these substitutions sound much better than others. Inform them that experience is the key, and that just because an idea may be theoretically correct doesn't necessarily mean it is the best choice from an artistic point of view.

Next, they'll need some altered chord fingerings, like the ones below.

ALTERED DOMINANT CHORDS

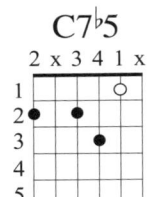 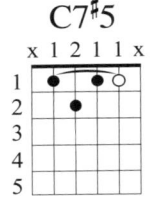 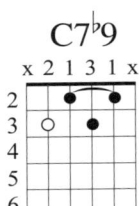 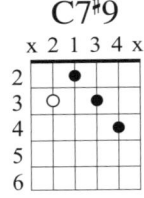 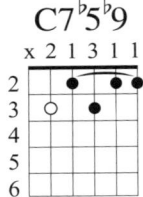 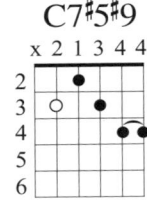 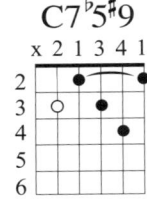 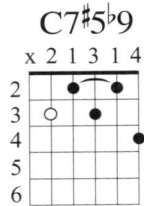

IMPROVISATION CONCEPTS

At first, you can take the same approach with jazz students as you did with beginning blues improvisers. When working with a new scale, let them explore the notes randomly while you play a backup progression. Later, introduce playing with all whole notes, half notes, etc. Then come the licks, melodic patterns and other tricks.

IMPROVISING WITH THE MAJOR SCALE

Even though improvising with the major scale isn't very exciting at first, it is important to guide your students through this very slowly. We apply many of the same concepts used with the major scale to other scales later on.

The major scale is a perfect vehicle for teaching topics such as arpeggios, upper and lower neighbor tones, finding melodic ideas, connecting ideas and so many others. Having your students apply these concepts to the major scale—until the information is firmly rooted—will make it much easier to apply them to other scales in the future.

ALTERED DOMINANT SCALES

Many jazz educators consider the following scales to be the most important for improvising over altered dominant chords. Be sure to explain why these scales work, and provide licks and other melodic ideas to get the point across. Some students don't like the sound of these scales at first. Tell them to keep practicing, as some of these sounds take a little "growing into."

Here are a couple of fingerings for each of these scales.

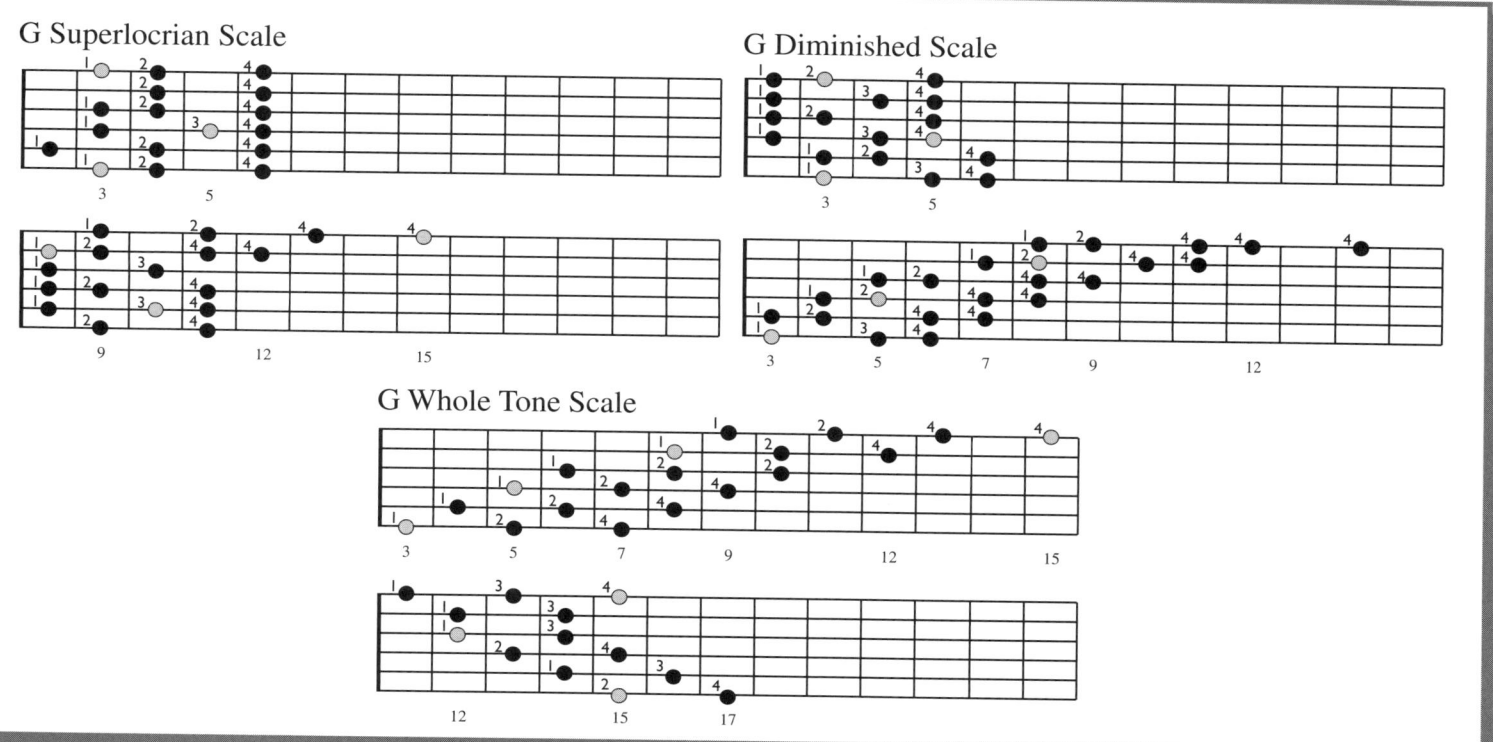

G Superlocrian Scale

G Diminished Scale

G Whole Tone Scale

Backing Track—*Bossa*

This is based on major (ii–V–I) and minor (ii°–V–i) changes.

Amin7 / D9 / GMaj7 / CMaj7 / F#min7♭5 / B7 / Emin7 / Emin7 /

Amin7 / D9 / GMaj7 / CMaj7 / F#min7♭5 / B7 / Emin7 / Emin7 /

F#min7♭5 / B7 / Emin7 / Emin7 / Amin7 / D9 / GMaj7 / CMaj7 /

F#min7♭5 / B7 / Emin7   E♭9 / Dmin7   D♭9 / CMaj7 / B7 / Emin7 / Emin7 //

Backing Track—*Rhythm Changes*

Here is a progression based on rhythm changes in B♭:

B♭Maj7   Gmin7 / Cmin7   F9   / B♭Maj7   Gmin7 / Cmin7   F9 /

Fmin7   B♭13 / E♭Maj7   E♭min7 / B♭Maj7   Gmin7 / Cmin7   F9 /

B♭Maj7   Gmin7 / Cmin7   F9   / B♭Maj7   Gmin7 / Cmin7   F9 /

Fmin7   B♭13 / E♭Maj7   E♭min7 / B♭Maj7   F9 /   B♭Maj7 /

D9 / D9 / G9 / G9 / C9 / C9 / F9 / F9 /

B♭Maj7   Gmin7 / Cmin7   F9   / B♭Maj7   Gmin7 / Cmin7   F9   /

Fmin7   B♭13   / E♭Maj7   E♭min7 / B♭Maj7   F9 / B♭Maj7 //

ARPEGGIOS

When your students start studying arpeggios, they will begin to see the bigger picture when it comes to improvisation.

First, have them memorize a set of diatonic arpeggios. There are many systems for this out there, or you could devise your own. The next steps are:

1. Have your students improvise using only arpeggio tones. First use one-chord vamps, then progressions.

2. Allow your students to improvise using entire scales again, but with each new phrase starting on a chord tone. Again, start with one-chord vamps, then go on to progressions.

This is a very natural way to add a more melodic sound and start to spell out the changes in solos. This takes time. Let your students know this.

Here are some diatonic arpeggios to get them started:

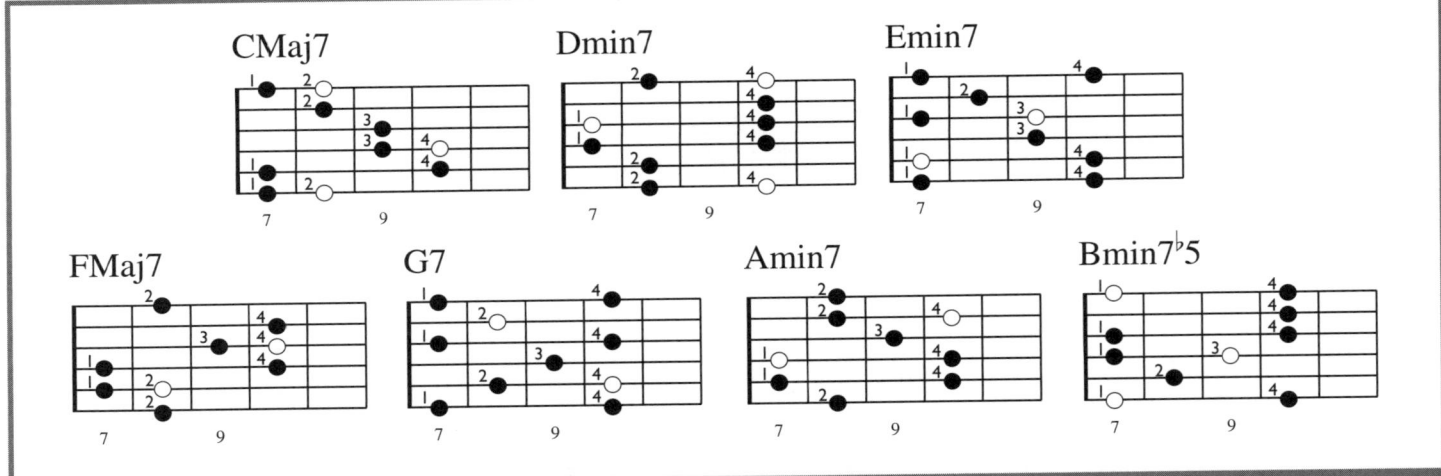

LICKS

Once again, give your students some licks in the beginning. This will accustom them to the jazz sound a little earlier. Here are some typical licks you can use:

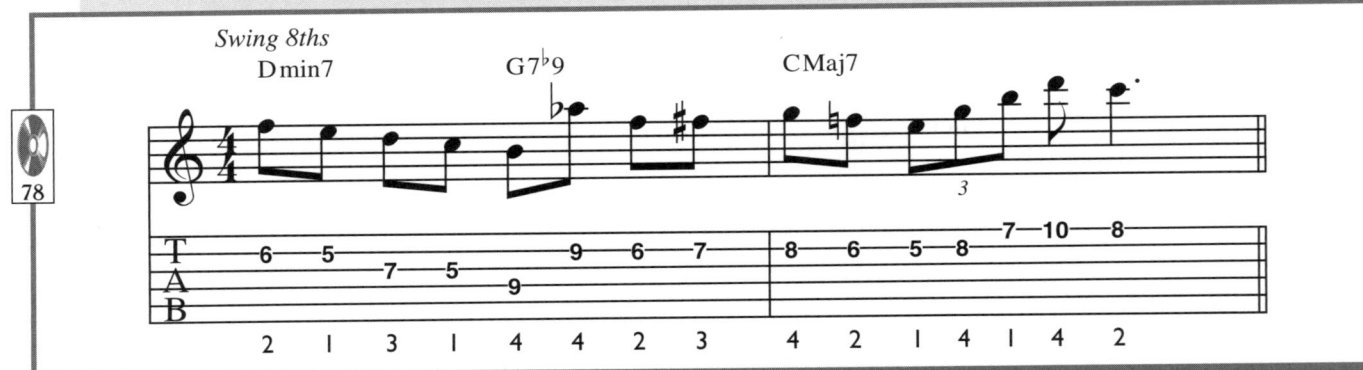

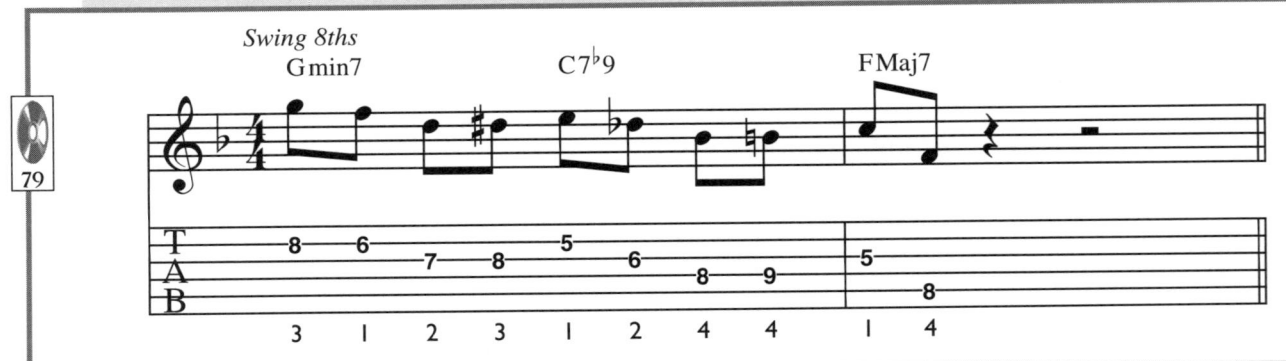

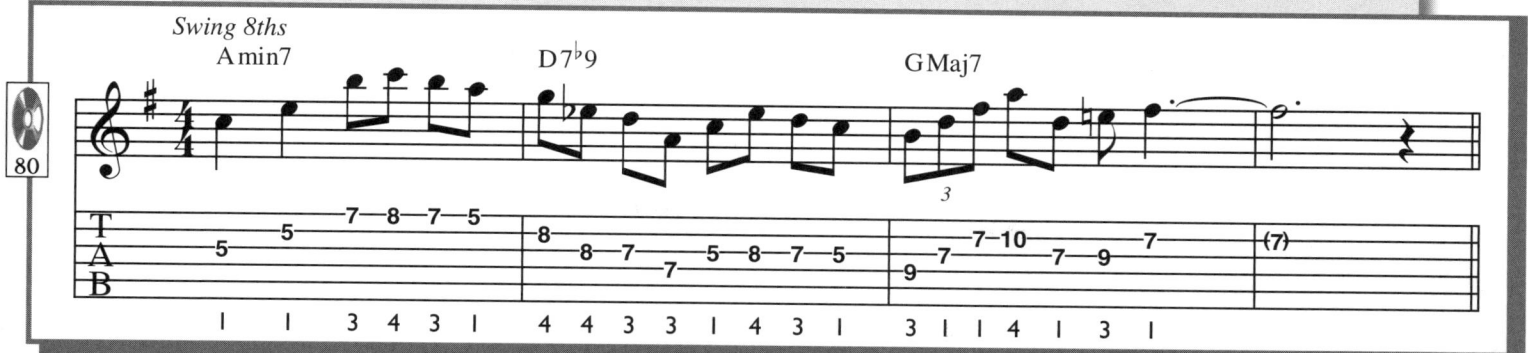

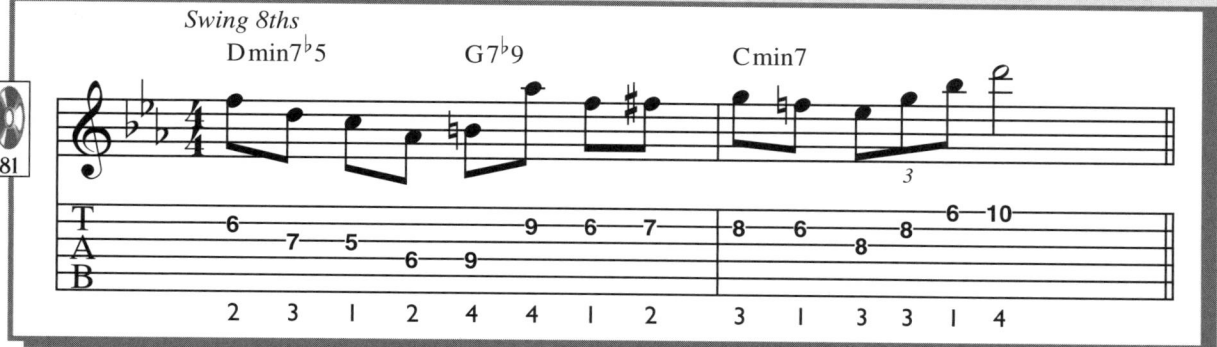

OTHER AREAS OF STUDY FOR JAZZ STUDENTS

- Jazz rhythms: swing, bossa, etc.
- Ear training
- Transcribing
- Jazz blues progressions
- "Rhythm changes" progressions
- Developing speed
- Becoming familiar with other common chord progressions in jazz
- Producing good tone
- Melodic development
- Chord substitution
- Re-harmonization

There is no end to the study of jazz. This list simply shows some of the things we must all work on, both as students and teachers.

REPERTOIRE DEVELOPMENT

As a jazz musician, you need to know hundreds, maybe thousands of songs. After certain theory fundamentals have been covered, it is best to use actual jazz tunes and standards as vehicles for acquiring more knowledge and skills. Too many teachers only teach theory and/or technique. We all started playing music because we wanted to play songs. Instead of filling a student's head with theory before many tunes are learned, try using songs to teach these things instead. This way your students end up knowing what they need to and have a lot of songs to play as well. Their sense of melody will be better when improvising, and their chord work will develop more tastefully.

Try to show them songs they will be playing with jazz groups and on future gigs. Show them how to transpose quickly and how to use their ear to catch the substitutions that may be used as well.

Final Thoughts

You now possess enough information to successfully make a living teaching guitar. *Your* best teacher will be experience, but this book should prove a valuable resource for you. The rewards to teaching are many. You can really have a positive impact on people's lives, while making a living doing something you love. Enjoy!

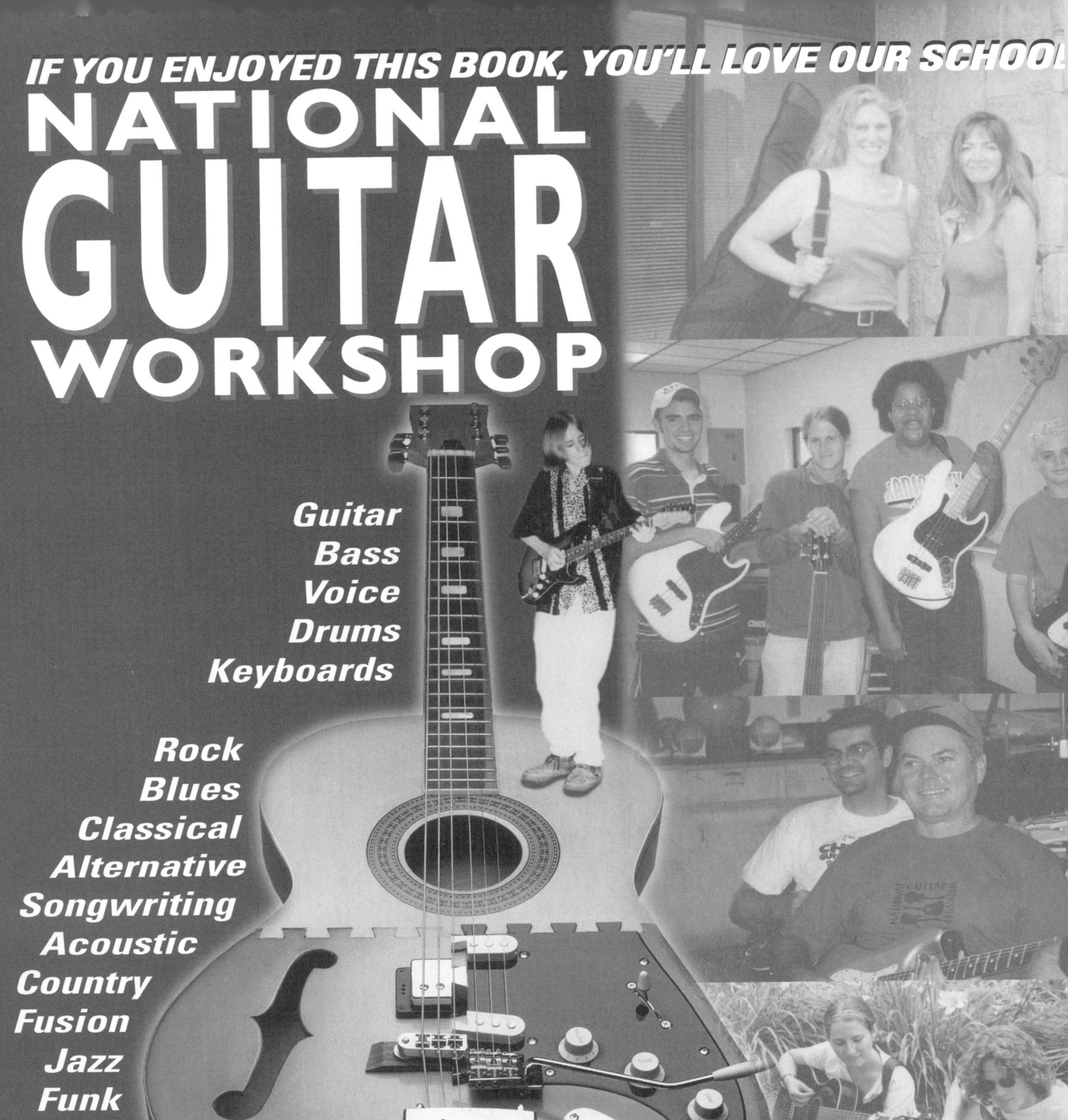